You Can Get There From Here:
A Story About Leadership

Phil Skramstad

Henle Printing Co.

Marshall, MN

Edited by: Mr. Dana Yost

ISBN: 978-0-615-18843-0

Printed in the United States of America

imarcltd.com

Forward

There are many books on leadership out there, but I thought there was a need for a leadership book that was uncomplicated and easy to understand for people at all levels in the corporate structure. I wanted to write a story that was engaging and conversational, yet got my message across. This book is the result.

The story and the characters are fictional, but their personalities and "leadership attributes" are combinations of several CEOs, managers, supervisors and front-line staff that I have met and worked with over the years.

I passionately believe that strong leadership is developed over years of experiences, mistakes, good mentorship, plus leadership training and development. I believe that natural born business leaders very rarely, if ever, exist. For the most part, I have found that there are people with great personal skills for leadership, and there are people with great technical skills for leadership; but the combination of both is very rare without being developed over time.

I hope you enjoy my story.

Phil Skramstad

"You Can Get There From Here"

Chapter I: "Yes, You Can!"

Ryan Michaels was sitting behind his desk with his head in his hands. He was exhausted. He was going over and over in his mind what he had done wrong – what he was doing wrong. The answer had to be there, but it wasn't coming.

He had been the CEO of Bedford Community Hospital for three years. The hospital had 375 employees and they weren't happy. Morale was at its lowest point since he had been there and he couldn't figure out why. The staff had quit smiling, his department managers were complaining, and BCH had just received its worst scores on the patient satisfaction surveys in the history of the hospital.

Things were going along so well when he first arrived. The hospital was in the top ten percent of the comparable hospital data on the patient satisfaction survey, the hospital seemed to be completely patient focused, it was profitable and the staff was happy.

It didn't take a genius to figure out that it was probably his fault. Things started going downhill within months of his arrival. He had his own way of doing things that had been successful at his previous hospital, so he was going to implement them here. After all, if they worked there, they'll work here.

When he first started making the changes, the managers and the staff were resistant, but he kept pushing them, and they finally saw things his way. He simply explained that where he came from, these processes worked well, so in a hospital that has been so successful like BCH, they'll work even better. He knew he was right. After all, he was the CEO.

Ryan had just gotten off the phone with his wife Ellen, and was recalling the conversation:
"I just don't think I can do it anymore, Ellen."
"What in the world are you talking about Ryan?" Ellen said.
"I just can't motivate my managers anymore. They can't motivate their staff, and the staff has quit trying to improve at all. Our patients aren't getting the kind of care this hospital has built a reputation on, and the hospital has suffered. We've lost money for ten consecutive months and the Board is starting to question my leadership. I really think I've burnt myself out. I'm working too hard."
"Ryan, this just doesn't sound like you. What do you want to do?" she asked.
Ryan felt he was on the verge of quitting. "Honey, I know where I want to take this hospital, but from what I see, I just don't think I can get there – not from where we are now."

Ryan was reflecting on the conversation, when a faint, deep voice from behind him said, "Yes, you can."

Completely startled, Ryan jumped up from his desk, almost fell over and looked behind him. There stood a very tall, thin man wearing a fringed suede leather jacket, leaning against the wall and smoking a cigarette. He had long white hair, slicked back in a ponytail. To Ryan, it didn't looked like he had shaved – or bathed – in a few days.

"Who in the heck are you and where did you come from?" yelled Ryan. "Put out that cigarette right now and get out of my office!" As soon as Ryan said it, the cigarette disappeared. But not the man.

Still startled, Ryan shouted, "How did you get into my office? Who are you? What are you doing here?"

The somewhat noble looking man in the suede jacket said, "Sorry about the cigarette, Ryan. I forget where I am sometimes. My name is Sammy."

Getting very angry, Ryan repeated, "I guess you didn't understand me! I asked you how you got into my office and what are you doing here?"

Sammy said, "Does it really make any difference how I got here, Ryan? You're my next assignment. I've been sent here to help you."

"Help me?" Ryan blurted out. "How can you help me! Look at yourself. You look like some old hippy from the '60s – or worse."

Sammy just smiled. "Trust me Ryan. I've helped many, many CEOs, managers and other leaders make it over the hump. You've just lost your way. Remember, you told your wife that even though you know where you wanted to take your hospital you didn't think you could get there. You CAN get there from here, Ryan. I will show you the way. You just have to have a little faith. Man, you just have to have a little trust."

Ryan's mind staggered. "Listen, Sammy whoever you are. I have a lot to do and I have a lot of problems. I don't need to be bothered right now by someone that I'm not even sure is real." Ryan thought he had completely lost his mind. He was now talking back to someone who couldn't possibly be in his office.

Sammy smiled softly again and said, "Ryan, you are not going crazy. I am real and I am here. All I ask is that you show a little faith and trust in me. You CAN get there from here. It will just take different leadership from you and your managers. Could you please show me the hospital's goals for this year?"

"Goals? Our goal is always to do as good as we can. Our goal is to take care of our patients." Ryan was almost screaming at him. "We don't need formal goals. We're a small hospital and we get along just fine. So please go away – if you're really there."

Sammy just shook his head. "Why do they always assign me the stubborn ones? They know I don't like to work that hard anymore, and this is going to take work." He was mumbling. "Ryan, we have a lot of work to do. So go home and get some sleep."

Curious now, Ryan said, "OK. I'll play along. Where do we start?"

Sammy smiled broadly and said, "We need a plan. That's where we start. So go home and think about BCH's future. Think about where you'd like your hospital to be three years from now and I will be back tomorrow at 3p.m. I'm in kind of a hurry, so I'll see you later."

"Where do you need to be in such a hurry?" Ryan was getting a bit mesmerized by this strange man.

Sammy started laughing. "Well, number one I really need a cigarette, and number two, the boys and I have a tee time at Augusta National. Can't miss that. Pretty tough course to get on."

And just that quick, Sammy was gone.

Chapter II: Worthwhile Work

At 3p.m. the next day, Ryan was sitting waiting in his office for someone that he was pretty sure was not real – part of an overworked, stressed imagination. The time came and went, and Ryan was actually relieved.

Ryan thought about what this guy Sammy had said. Maybe he was right about the goals. Ryan remembered a few years back that the Board of Directors did a strategic plan with the long-range goals for the hospital. After the plan was received, he put it away and hadn't looked at it since. Maybe he would try to find it and give it a look. But what for, he thought. He would do things his way. They worked before and they will work again.

At 3:10p.m., the deep voice from behind him said, "Sorry I'm late."

Again startled, Ryan jumped and said, "You have to stop doing that. You're going to give me a heart attack!"

"Well," Sammy said, "at least you're in a good place if that is going to happen."

"So, I guess you are real. You're not going to be a very good coach if you keep showing up late."

Sammy smiled. "I said I was sorry, but I had to have a cigarette first. Not only that, it was my turn to make the tee time. We're playing Pebble Beach this afternoon. Do you know how tough it is to get a tee time there?"

"Number one," Ryan said in a definite irritated voice, "you should quit smoking, and number two, I could care less about golf. It's a waste of time."

Sammy just looked at Ryan. "So, are you on board? Are you going to allow me to show you how you can get where you want to go, or are you just going to sit there and complain about my bad habits?"

Ryan thought for a moment and then said, "I'll make a deal with you. You quit smoking and stop talking about golf, and I will agree to listen to what you have to say."

Sammy frowned. "You're asking quite a bit. I have smoked for longer than you'd ever believe. And golf is my passion."

"Take it or leave it," Ryan said.

Sammy said nothing for what seemed to Ryan to be an eternity. Finally he said, "You win. Let's get to work."

"What's first?" Ryan couldn't believe he was actually excited about this extremely strange circumstance.

"Worthwhile work." Sammy said immediately.

"Worthwhile work? What are you talking about?" Ryan was puzzled.

"Ryan, tell me what you do here. What do you do at this hospital?"

Ryan almost laughed. "That's pretty easy. We heal people. We save lives. We try to make our patients and their families as comfortable as we can. Why?"

Sammy smiled, but was agitated. He was getting down to business and he needed a cigarette. "Would you say what you do, then, is worthwhile? Do you think you make a difference?"

"Of course we do!"

Sammy continued to ask the questions. "Does everyone play a part in what you said, or is it just certain departments?"

Ryan thought for a moment and then said, "Well, not everyone gets to see the patients – or their families – but I guess in a way they all play a part in what the patient gets. They all have a role in our success."

"Exactly! So really, every department does incredible worthwhile work, don't they?" Sammy really wanted a cigarette. "Tell me the last time you told your department heads how important what they do is to the success of this hospital and in your vision of healing people and saving lives."

Ryan kind of scoffed, but said, "Sammy, I think they know. They're smart people and they do their jobs well. That isn't the problem."

"So your answer is that you haven't told them?"

"Listen Sammy, I have more important things to do. If this is all you have for me, you might as well go."

"Ryan, just hear me out. People like to know that they're making a difference. They like to know that what they do means something. Yes, you're probably right that deep down they know, but they need to hear it. Working in a hospital can be depressing some days and attitudes can really suffer. These people need to know that they matter and that they really make a difference. By hearing it often, it can generate enthusiasm. Enthusiasm generates positive attitudes, and positive attitudes help us all to work smarter and can actually improve our performance. Some days, attitude is everything."

Sammy continued: "Ryan, your department managers need to hear that. It all starts with you, and then it continues with them. They also need to know that communicating their worthwhile work to their staff is just as important to keep the enthusiasm and attitudes positive in their department. Every department. From Nursing and Surgery, to Housekeeping and Maintenance. Everyone contributes. Everyone plays a part, and they need to hear it – often. Also Ryan, make sure that you are specific. Tell them exactly how they make a difference when you praise them."

Ryan was paying attention now. "I guess I never really thought about it like that. We get so busy around here that I think sometimes we forget that very basic idea that we do make a difference."

Sammy was smiling again, but still craved a cigarette. "So, what are you going to do about it?"

Ryan thought for a moment. "Well, we have a managers meeting tomorrow morning. That will be the first thing on my agenda."

"Your agenda?" Sammy asked. "Is it always your agenda?"

"Of course. Why?"

Sammy looked at his watch. "That will have to wait for another time. I have to go. Tee time you know. You work on this first step and I will see you in two weeks. Same time."

"But what about my plan, my roadmap? You told me to think about where I would like this hospital to be three years from now."

"Don't worry, Ryan. We'll get there."

"Remember your promise, Sammy. No smoking."

Sammy frowned, and was gone.

****

The next morning at 7:30a.m., Ryan called the meeting to order of the entire leadership team of the Bedford Community Hospital. For once, all of the managers were there.

Ryan started out, "We have a lot of things to cover this morning, but first I want to ask you: What do we do here?" They all just looked at each other with that "what's this all about" look.

Ann, the Director of Nursing started out by saying "That's pretty obvious isn't it, Mr. Michaels? We tend to our patients."

"Yes, you're right, Ann. That's what **you** do. And you and your team do it very well. Do you think it's important? You know, worthwhile?"

Ann just stared at him. "Of course it is! Without us, this hospital would fail." The rest of the managers just rolled their eyes. "Here she goes again," they were thinking.

Ryan smiled. She was going just where he thought she would. "Yes Ann, you're right again. The Nursing team plays an important part. Very patient focused and without you and your team, we wouldn't succeed." Now the other managers were starting to get upset, even flustered; but Ryan continued, "But remember Ann, it's only one role. It is extremely important, but could we survive without Housekeeping?"

Ann thought for a moment. "I see your point. Without them, the hospital wouldn't be clean and sterile. The patient's health could suffer and visitors could come down with an infection. Not only that, the appearance would create a really bad perception for those who come here. I guess their role is important."

Linda, the Housekeeping Manager was beaming. She said, "I didn't think anyone really appreciated all we go through."

"Yes Linda," Ryan said, "what you do is extremely important to the success of this hospital. Extremely worthwhile."

For the next hour, Ryan went around the table and discussed the worthwhile work of all of the departments: Maintenance, Business Office, Laundry, Dietary, Human Resources – all of them. The discussion was actually spirited and everyone perked up. Attitudes were good.

Ryan finally said, "I think the important thing to remember is that we all contribute to our success. What we all do in our departments is incredibly worthwhile. Don't you think it's about time that we start respecting all of our roles a little more? Say 'thank you' to each other for each of our contributions. We are a team. We need to depend on each other and we need to improve our service to each other. When we have a goal or a problem, we should solve it together because more than one department can be affected. Actually we all affect each other." Ryan continued because he could see they were listening for a change. "It all starts here with each of us. We have to inspire our own teams to do the same."

"How do we do that, Mr. Michaels?" Jim from Maintenance finally spoke up. Ryan was thinking that this was one of the first times Jim had ever said anything in one of these meetings. Jim continued, "You know as well as I do that morale here is pretty low. I know my staff is doing their job, but they're just going through the motions. They don't seem to care too much and I don't know what to do."

Ryan smiled. His perceptions were right, after all. Morale was low and maybe, just maybe, Sammy was right. Maybe this is the place to start.

"Well Jim," started Ryan, "you start with doing the same thing with your team that we did today. At your next team meeting, discuss the work that you do in your department, and how it all contributes to the success of this hospital. You know that without the work you do in Maintenance that this hospital would go down the tubes very quickly. Approach it like that and discuss how worthwhile what they do is. As a new friend of mine just told me, people like to know that what they do really makes a difference. It motivates them; makes them feel good about themselves. Jim, remember to also talk about what the other departments do and how they contribute. Show them that it is important to respect the work of the other departments. Tell them to thank their co-workers in the other departments - that they will appreciate it."

He continued. "And always remember to be specific as to what the praise is for. Don't just say 'thanks, great job.' They need to know exactly what you are praising them for – exactly what they do that makes such a big difference."

Ryan looked at the rest of the managers: "That goes for all of you. I want you all to have this same meeting with your teams."

Stephanie from Physical Therapy finally said, "What about you, Mr. Michaels?"

"What about me, Stephanie?"

Stephanie continued, "What you do is really important too. Who's going to thank you?"

Ryan smiled widely. "You just did Stephanie. Yes, I think I understand that what I do is important to our success, but I also understand better than ever that my job is just a role, too. I can't do my job without all of you and your teams. It's that simple."

Doris from the Business Office whispered to Ann, "Wow, I never thought I'd see the day where I heard that."

Ryan heard the comment, but said nothing. He looked at his watch and couldn't believe the time. They had been there for two hours and didn't get past the first item on the agenda. It was scheduled to be a two-hour meeting, and he wasn't going to keep them any longer.

"I think that will be it for today," he said. "I thought it was important that we had this discussion. Everything else can wait, but we will have a special one-hour meeting in two days at the same time to finish the agenda. Thanks for listening."

****

Over the next few days, Ryan noticed a change in attitudes from his Directors. They seemed more inspired. It was a small change, but Ryan couldn't help but wonder whether his meeting with them was the reason. Could it be Sammy was right?

He met Ann in the hallway that afternoon. As Ann passed him, she had a big smile on her face as she said "Good afternoon Mr. Michaels. How is your day going?"

"I'm really good, Ann. You seem to be in a cheerful mood."

"I am. Some of my nurses seem to have a new sense of purpose. I did what you said. I sat down with all of them in the last two days and had the conversation about worthwhile work, and you were right! They are all smart people and I know they knew that their work could be life-changing for the patients, but I don't think they had ever thought about it before. Once I brought it up, and many of them really understood what a difference they make in the lives of our patients and how they contributed to our success, they seemed to start working with a new inspiration – at least for now. So, Mr. Michaels, if I seem to be in a cheerful mood as you put it, I am. Any time my nurses are happy, I'm happy."

"You said only some of them felt that way," Ryan asked. "What about the rest of them?"

Ann explained. "You know as well as I do, Mr. Michaels, that any time someone brings up something different, or people get a little out of their routine, that change is difficult for some. Actually, for some, change is not a possibility. There will always be skeptics. As leaders we can only do as much as we possibly can to affect that change. We just need to get them all of the information."

"Good job, Ann." Ryan had to remember to recognize his team like that more often. Too often, he thought, he forgot the simple things. Like telling his team when they're doing well. The first thing he was going to do when he got back to his office was to put "team recognition" at the top of his to-do list – every day. Ann was a good leader, Ryan thought. He could learn a little from her. He must listen more.

****

As the next week passed, Ryan noticed that same sense of purpose with all of his managers. This couldn't be that easy, he thought. Communicating worthwhile work he knew now was important, but that couldn't be the answer to all of BCH's issues. Yet as he walked around his hospital throughout that whole week, he even noticed most of the staff seemed to be working harder. They seemed to be happier and smiling more. Wait until he saw Sammy again. If Sammy kept his word, that would be in three more days.

The day before Sammy was scheduled to meet with Ryan, he met Ann again in the hallway. This time she wasn't smiling or as cheerful as he had noticed over the past week. This time she passed him and didn't say a word.

"Ann," he said stopping her. "What's wrong? Where's that cheerful attitude you've had the past few weeks?"

"Well," she frowned, "my team is at it again. That great attitude and inspired work lasted about five minutes! I guess a little longer than that, but that same bad morale is back. I don't know what I did wrong, Mr. Michaels." There were tears in her eyes. "I thought everything was great, but I was wrong. I thought communicating that worthwhile work was the answer. It was working. But now, I just don't know. Sorry."

Ryan was stunned. He thought it was the answer, too. He knew it couldn't be that easy. Maybe Sammy wasn't the genius Ryan had begun to think he was. Which made Ryan start to think again. Who was this guy? How was he getting into my office without anyone noticing? He even started to think that maybe it was all a dream and that he really was losing it.

Hopefully, the answers will come tomorrow afternoon. That's when Sammy said he was going to be there again. Sure, Ryan thought. And I'll win the lottery!

Chapter III: "How Do You Lead Them"?

The next afternoon Ryan was catching up on work in his office. He had put this off for too long and he was way behind. What a mess, he thought. "My desk looks like a garbage dump. I really have to start keeping my desk in order. Maybe a daily to-do list would work. I really have to start prioritizing some of this stuff or none of it will get done."

Ryan continued to do his work when he started to hear a smacking sound coming from behind him. He stopped working and listened. Smack. Pop. Smack. Pop.

"What in the world is that?" Ryan mumbled. I wonder if it could be that darn air conditioner again, he thought. I'll have to give Jim a call and have him look at it. The noise kept on and he couldn't concentrate anymore. He picked up the phone to give Jim a call and looked toward the noise.

And there he was.

There was Sammy, leaning against the wall. Startled again just for that moment, Ryan jumped up and said "Sammy, you can't do that! Are you making that terrible sound?"

"Sorry, Ryan. Didn't mean to scare you. And yes, that noise was me chewing my bubble gum." Sammy looked deep in thought for a second and then said, "I didn't know a person could make such big bubbles with this stuff."

"Sammy," Ryan said as he started to pace, "I don't really know why, but I'm really glad to see you. I have so many questions, but first of all, why in the world are you chewing bubble gum? It's really annoying."

Somewhat testily, Sammy said "Do you have any idea how tough it is to quit smoking?' I had to do something. I made you a promise and I intend to keep it. So don't bug me, all right?"

It was Ryan's turn to smile. "So, you quit smoking then?"

Sammy looked a bit sheepish. "Well, if you don't count when I play golf, than yes, I have."

"Sammy, everything counts. You can't just do something when it suits you. If you're going to quit, then quit."

Now Sammy was pacing. "I'm trying. Really. It's not as easy as you think. The gum helps a little, but not when I hit a bad shot on the golf course."

"Hey Sammy, change is tough for everyone, but you simply have to stick to it. You have to change your habits in order to change your behavior. Keep a positive attitude about it and the change will happen."

Sammy smiled broadly and said: "Exactly!"

"What's that supposed to mean?" Ryan asked.

"It'll come to you," Sammy said.

Ryan finally sat down at his desk and pointed at Sammy. "Sit down. I have a lot of questions for you. I wasn't so sure you were going to show up – heck, I didn't even know if you were real – but now that you're here, you have a lot of questions to answer."

Sammy sunk himself in the chair across from Ryan's desk. He popped in another piece of bubble gum, crossed his legs and said: "OK, shoot."

"First of all, how do you get in here? My assistant always lets me know when someone is here for me, and she would never let someone walk in unannounced. How do you get by her?"

"Maybe she doesn't see me." Sammy smiled. "Look Ryan, does it really make that much difference to you? I agreed to help you through your crisis, and if I can deliver, does it really matter? As long as I do what I say I can do for you, can't you overlook my little idiosyncrasies?"

Ryan thought for a second. "Showing up unannounced is very rude, Sammy. As long as you don't pop in when I have someone in my office, I guess I can overlook it. Just be here when you say you're going to be here. Don't be late!"

"Ryan, I would never barge in when you have someone in your office, and I will be on time. Next question."

Ryan cocked his head to one side and looked at Sammy. "Who are you?"

Again, Sammy just smiled. "I told you. My name is Sammy and I've been sent here to help you."

"By who?"

"I've been sent by people who are concerned about you; by people who know that you have what it takes, but have lost your way. I've been sent by people who honestly know that you can get there...from here." Sammy was tapping his finger on Ryan's desk as he was saying it.

"So," Ryan smiled, "the Board hired you." It was a statement, not a question.

Sammy started laughing. "No, the Board didn't hire me, Ryan. Let's get to some important questions. Remember, I have promised to help you. I keep my promises, so beyond that, it doesn't make any difference who hired me or where I came from."

"Sounds a little fishy, but OK." Ryan relented, but was not satisfied. He would find out – sooner or later. "But I have another question."

"One more, Ryan. Then we should move on."

Ryan started in. "I had that meeting with my managers. You know, the one about worthwhile work? We spent two hours on it, and by the end of my meeting, it was great. My managers understood and they really felt good about what they did."

Ryan continued. "During the next ten days or so, I noticed a change – especially in Ann's department. I noticed the change in attitude not only with my managers, but also with many of the staff. They seemed to be working with a better attitude and with a purpose. So naturally, I thought we had found the answer to the low morale – worthwhile work. Then a few days ago, it stopped. Things went back to the way they were before I started talking about it. What happened? What did I do wrong?"

Chapter III: "How Do You Lead Them?"

"First of all, Ryan," Sammy started, "the answer to low morale and quality work isn't a one-issue answer. Communicating worthwhile work is extremely important, but it's just one piece of the puzzle. It's not the end-all. And Ryan, you didn't do anything wrong. You just didn't do enough."

"What do you mean?" Ryan asked.

"Let me ask you a question, Ryan. Once you had the meeting with the managers about worthwhile work, did you bring it up again?"

"Well, no I didn't." Ryan looked puzzled. "I didn't see the need to. After all, we spent two hours on it in the meeting. I thought that should be more than enough time to devote to it."

Sammy smiled. "Ryan, change is tough for some, but you have to stick to it. People need reinforcement constantly. In order to change their attitude, you have to first change their behavior. In order to change their behavior, you have to first change their habits – in this case how they think; how they perceive the way they work. Does any of this sound familiar?"

Ryan just rolled his eyes and nodded.

Sammy continued. "Worthwhile work takes constant communication. People that have worked one way for so long and thought a certain way about what they do for so long have to be reminded constantly that what they do is significant – important. That way, it has a chance to spread throughout the entire hospital. That's how you change behavior and attitude. That's how you change a culture."

"I think I get it now." Ryan nodded. "It can't be a one-time push, so to speak. It has to be forever. There has to be continuous follow-up."

"Now you get it," Sammy smiled. "It's just like the staff training you do, Ryan. If that's all there is, it ultimately does no good; it ultimately has no value. There must always be continuous follow-up on any initiatives. Otherwise, why do it?"

Ryan was listening now. This guy – whoever he was – seemed to make a lot of sense. Ryan would start again tomorrow on this initiative. Worthwhile work will – must – become a part of BCH's culture. It was a good idea. It was the right thing to do.

Sammy looked at his watch. "We still have a few things to cover in today's session, so let's move on. I have a tee time at...."

Ryan interrupted. "Sammy! You promised!"

"You're right. Sorry. Let's just say that we're on a schedule. One more question. How do you manage your managers? Let me put it a different way. How do you lead them?"

"Interesting question, Sammy", Ryan started. "I really don't feel that I have to lead them. After all, they were put into their positions because of their skills. They really know more about their jobs and day-to-day tasks than I do. I just tell them what to do, and then they report back to me what they did. I think that's the right thing to do. I certainly don't want to micro-manage them."

Sammy cocked his head to one side and didn't say anything for a minute. Then, "Ryan, do you do that with all of your managers?"

"Of course," Ryan said. "I want to be fair. I want to treat them all the same."

"Are they all long-term managers?"

"No they're not. As a matter of fact, Lisa, the Lab Manager, just started last month."

"So then," Sammy continued to ask the questions, "Lisa is managed the same way? You let her make the decisions about her department the same as the rest?"

Ryan raised his voice just enough that Sammy noticed. He was getting a little testy, Sammy thought. "Of course I do! I hired Lisa because of her skills. She did an outstanding job as a Lab employee. One of the best we ever had. So when our former Lab Manager moved, I thought of Lisa immediately. There wasn't a doubt in by mind."

"One more thing about Lisa, Ryan. Had she ever had any management experience before? Had she ever managed people? And how is the morale and attitude in her department?"

Now Ryan was shouting. "No she hadn't, Sammy! But like I said, she is very talented. She'll be fine. As far as her staff goes, they're no different than the rest right now. Morale is low and attitudes are bad. So get off my case!"

Sammy was deep in thought. "Ryan, I know you made a lot of changes when you first got here. How did that go?"

Ryan was steaming. "If you must know, not very well at first, but once I explained that the changes worked at my last hospital so they were going to work here, they adjusted."

"Did you tell them why it was important – why it was worthwhile - or did you just tell them to do it?"

Ryan just glared at Sammy. "I just told them to do it. Listen, smart guy, I know what I'm doing."

"OK, Ryan. One last question about these changes you made. Did you show them how you wanted the processes changed? After all, it was new to them."

Ryan started shouting again. "Sammy, I told you before, these people are smart. I don't want to micro-manage them. That's not me! It didn't make any difference to show them how I wanted it done. I simply told them to do it. And they got it done!"

"Calm down Ryan," Sammy said in a very calm, soft voice, "Have you ever heard of the book 'Leadership and the One Minute Manager'* by Dr. Ken Blanchard?"

Ryan thought for a second. "I have heard of the book, but I haven't read it; and I certainly have heard of Blanchard. Who hasn't?"

Sammy produced the book out of his backpack and handed it to Ryan. "Ryan, I want you to do me a favor. Humor me and read the book. It won't take you too long. I'll be back in two weeks at the same time and we'll talk about what you thought of it. OK?" Sammy started getting up from his chair and then said "Oh Ryan, one more thing for you to think about. Who ran your last managers meeting?"

*Leadership and the One Minute Manager," by Ken Blanchard, Patricia Zigarmi and Drea Zigarmi

Ryan was quickly losing his patience. "Like I told you before Sammy, I run the meetings. I'm the CEO. I set the agendas – it's my job."

"Always?" Sammy asked.

"Always!" Ryan shouted back.

"Just give it some thought, Ryan. And please read the book."

Ryan quickly thumbed through the book. "I guess I can do that, but I'm not sure what you're trying to get at. I think I've been a good boss. I've read leadership books before and some of them are OK, but I choose to do things my way. It's worked pretty well for quite a while."

When he was done talking, Ryan looked up at Sammy, but the chair was empty. Sammy was gone.

Chapter IV: "What Do You Think Now?"

Over the next few weeks, Ryan read Dr. Blanchard's book. It certainly was about managing a different way than he was used to. The book talked about leading people according to their skills and commitment on any particular task – on any particular job. It said that you shouldn't lead all people the same way because they all don't have the same skills or the same commitment to do their job. It talked about actually leading the same person several different ways depending on the particular task they were doing.

It made some sense to Ryan, but he didn't think it was that relevant. Not in his case. He was quite comfortable managing his team the way he was currently leading them, and he didn't see any reason to change. It just didn't seem fair to his managers to treat them differently. If nothing else, Ryan was fair. He didn't treat any of his managers differently than the others. He showed no favoritism and he wasn't about to start now.

He thought it was only appropriate that, because he was the CEO, he could direct his staff to carry out his ideas the way they wanted to – as long as it got done. After all, they were managers. They should know what it takes. It's not like they have to do all of the work themselves. They have staff that they can delegate some of the work to. Ryan thought that it was all about the direction. Tell people what you want done and then let them do it. He didn't think all of this nonsense about training, showing, telling, and observing people was necessary. It was a waste of time. After all, people wouldn't have been hired unless they knew what to do. They wouldn't have been hired without the necessary skills, so telling them what to do and how to do it seemed to demean them. He wasn't going to fall into Sammy's little trap this time! He would show him a thing or two the next time he saw Sammy.

Ryan was thinking about all of this as he was walking down the hallway to his office. Once he got to his reception area, he stopped to talk to his Administrative Assistant, Donna.

"Hi Donna, any messages?"

"Actually no, Mr. Michaels. It's been fairly quiet. No phone calls, and no one has stopped in to see you," Donna said.

"Great!" Ryan said. "I have a lot of work to catch up on, so if there are any calls for me, just take a message. And if anyone does stop in to see me, have them make an appointment for later this afternoon. Thanks."

Ryan opened the door to his office…and there he was. Ryan stopped dead in his tracks and closed the door. There was Sammy leaning against Ryan's desk. His arms were crossed and he had a sucker in his mouth.

"Hello, Ryan. You're late!" Sammy said with a huge smile on his face. He continued, "You told me never to be late again, so look who's late this time."

Somewhat flustered, Ryan said, "I guess I lost track of the time, but you did it again! How did you get into my office without going past Donna? She said no one had been in."

Sammy just smiled and said, "Ryan, some day you will have that answer. I promise."

"So," Ryan grinned, "you promise that you will tell me at some point?"

"That's not exactly what I said, Ryan. What I said was that I promise that some day you will have the complete answer to exactly who I am. But not right now. Right now we have work to do, and a conversation to have about leadership."

"Yeah, I read the book," Ryan said somewhat reluctantly. And then he added, "What's the deal with the sucker?"

Sammy laughed. "The deal – as you put it – with the sucker is that the bubble gum didn't work. It worked for a while, but then I went back to my old habit. Started when I was playing golf last week at Carnoustie. I didn't play very well, so I smoked a lot more. Now I just smoke more than I ever did, so I thought I'd try the suckers. It worked for one of my golf buddies." Sammy sounded really frustrated.

Ryan just looked at him. This guy could really talk the talk, but when it came down to changing his own behavior and setting some goals, he couldn't perform. "Sounds to me like you have to take a look in the mirror, Sammy."

Sammy looked a bit surprised. "What do you mean?"

"Well, Sammy, for a guy that seems to have all of the answers you can't seem to come up with the answers for yourself. You talk a lot about worthwhile work and goals and changing behaviors. Isn't quitting smoking about all of those things?"

Sammy just stared at Ryan. "I'm listening."

Ryan continued. "What could be more worthwhile than quitting smoking? It's not healthy, it smells and it affects others. I'm sure it requires great willpower – I hear it's very addictive – so don't you have to really look at your own behavior? Sammy, take a look at the times you do smoke and be more conscious about changing those habits. Set a goal for goodness sake. Promise yourself you are going to quit smoking by a set date and stick to it."

Ryan was on a roll now, so he kept going. "Put a plan in place to make sure you quit smoking by that date. How can I continue to listen to someone about leadership, worthwhile work and goals when he apparently doesn't even understand those things himself?"

Sammy was grinning broadly now. "You know Ryan, you're right, and you surprised me. This may be easier with you than I originally thought. Thanks for the lecture. You kicked me pretty good, and I deserved it."

"What did you mean when you said this may be easier than you thought?" Ryan questioned.

"You'll understand completely through the next weeks, Ryan. A lot of what you just said when you scolded me is all about more effective leadership. I just meant that I think you'll be very coachable."

"If you're talking about that leadership book I just read," Sammy scowled, "I think you're mistaken. I just don't buy it!"

Sammy continued to lean against Ryan's desk, folded his arms again and asked, "And why is that, Ryan?"

Ryan started in. "Sammy, I have a very appropriate leadership style for my people. I don't tell them what to do. I think that is very demeaning. I give them a project - or a task, as the book says

– and I let them do it their way. It has worked just fine. No complaints from anyone. And how about this talk about motivating your employees and their attitudes? I just don't think you can do that! A boss can't control someone's motivation or attitude. That has to come from within."

He continued. "These are smart people I work with. They know their jobs. After all Sammy, this is a small hospital. I really don't think we need to lead our people with all of this mumbo-jumbo leadership from all of these books that are out there." Ryan thought he was on a roll now. He thought he was telling Sammy a thing or two, and he knew he was right.

Sammy just continued to lean against Ryan's desk and listen. He was smiling now – almost a smirk on his face – which really irritated Ryan.

Ryan started to pace, and he continued to lecture Sammy. "And I just don't buy all of this stuff about using different leadership styles depending on the situation. The book even went so far as saying you should use different leadership styles on the same person. What kind of logic is that? There's enough confusion around here without having to deal with that! Just think how some of my managers would react if I lead them one way, and then all of a sudden – just because it was a different task – started to lead them another way? No, I think my way is better. There's no way I will change the way I lead my staff. I'm comfortable with it, and so are they. End of story."

"Not the end of the story," Sammy said as he pointed his finger at Ryan. "In that whole discourse, you were right about one thing."

"And what's that?" Ryan was glaring at Sammy.

Sammy continued. "You said that a leader couldn't control a person's motivation or attitude. You were right about that. But, although you can't control their motivation, you can affect it by the way you lead. Part of your job is to inspire people to be better; to want to be better. And you can't do that if you lead them all the same way."

Now it was Sammy's turn to pace, and he continued. "I'd like to ask you a question, Ryan. Let's take your assistant, Donna. Do you think she has the same technical abilities in everything that you delegate to her?"

"Of course not!" Ryan threw up his hands. "She struggles with some of the things, but she eventually catches on."

"How about her motivation to do everything that you give her to do. Do you think she's just as passionate about all of them?"

"You know she isn't. What's the point?"

"The point, Ryan, is how can you possibly lead someone the same way in all of their tasks when their skills and motivation are different depending on the task? Our job as leaders is to give our people all of the tools and resources necessary to be successful in their job. If we always continue to make assumptions that they'll eventually get it, what kind of message are we sending them? Actually, we are setting them up, ultimately, to fail, aren't we?"

"Go on." Ryan suddenly wanted to hear more.

"OK Ryan, you said you read the book, right?"

Ryan nodded.

"Then you should understand that people's abilities and desire to do certain tasks are different. That's where affecting their motivation and attitude come in – by the way we lead them on those different tasks. If someone's desire to do something is low, we have to give them more encouragement. If someone's ability to do a task is low, we have to give them more information and more training. Don't you see, people feel good about themselves when they know they are doing a good job, and they feel better about their work when they are encouraged and recognized for getting it right – or in some cases, getting it almost right."

"You're starting to sound like the book," Ryan chuckled.

"Maybe so, but it makes sense. Isn't it our job to make sure all of the managers are winners? Isn't it our job to make sure all of the managers have the tools and skills necessary to lead their teams? Tell me something. When you tell any of your managers to get something done, do you know for sure they have the skills to do it, or are you just assuming they do? And Ryan, do you give them the 'why' part of it? Do you tell them why it is important; why it is worthwhile?"

A light bulb went on for Ryan. "Worthwhile work!"

"Exactly, Ryan. Don't ever keep them in the dark. They need to have all of the information relevant to their job, and their department. They need to know how everything affects them and the hospital in general. If you don't give them that information, how will they be able to give it to their staff? It all starts with you, and trickles throughout the whole organization."

"I guess I see your point," Ryan relented. "I guess I knew all along that it all made sense, but I've been doing the same things the same way for so long that I think I was a little bit scared."

"That's to be expected, Ryan," Sammy said as he put his hand on Ryan's shoulder. "And you'll make some mistakes along the way. Heck, if you don't make some mistakes, you're not even trying. This method of leadership has withstood the test of time, Ryan. It's very straightforward and it's a leadership development that you can start today."

Ryan threw up his hands. "Where do I start? My assumption is that all of my managers have the ability to do their jobs. My assumption has been that they can motivate themselves. So if I've been doing it wrong for all of this time, how can I possibly go back and correct it?"

Sammy just smiled. "It's not that tough, Ryan. You can start by meeting with each one individually and diagnosing their development levels on their job responsibilities."

Ryan got a funny look on his face. "Diagnosing them?"

"Yeah," Sammy said. "Isn't that a great word for a hospital? I think it's great!"

"So how do I do that?"

"Ask them; but a word of caution. Don't use the words from the book. Don't ask them about their competence and commitment on any particular task. They probably wouldn't take kindly to asking about their competence. Use other words. For competence, use words like experience, knowledge, skills; and for commitment, use words like confidence and desire. It'll go a lot better that way."

"Then what?"

"Well" Sammy continued, "then you can use the information from your book to determine how you will lead them. Like I said, you may end up leading the same person two, three, even four different ways. And for sure, you'll end up leading some of the managers completely different than you have been. You know, Ryan, one of the things us leaders love to do the best is make assumptions. We make assumptions because it takes less time and it's easy. But Ryan, we will never become truly effective leaders unless we take the time up front to make sure we are leading our staff the right way. In the long run, we are making winners out of them. And Ryan, if they win, you win! Any questions?"

"I sure do!" Ryan couldn't wait. "Let's say I discover that I am leading one of my managers completely different than I should be, so I decide to lead them differently. Won't that confuse them?"

Sammy just laughed. "The only way it will confuse them is if you don't tell them not only how you're going to lead them, but why. Repeat back to them what they told you about their development level and then say, 'based on what you told me, here's what I'm going to do and why'."

Ryan looked disappointed now. "So I won't be able to completely delegate tasks to my managers anymore?"

"Of course you will, Ryan. You just need to make sure that it is the appropriate leadership style based on their development level on that task. Always remember, Ryan; You should delegate everything that is appropriate. Nothing more, nothing less. One more thing Ryan; communicate with them often about how they are doing. Be interested in their success. Encourage them, support them and recognize them – often. Every day."

"Never once in all of my travels have I walked into any organization and have seen a sign that says: 'Stop Recognizing Me! Too Much Of That Going On Here!" Sammy started to laugh. "Pretty funny, huh?"

Ryan just looked down at the floor, deep in thought, and then said, "Sammy, I'll give it try. But I'm not making any promises. You have made a pretty good case, but I don't think my way was so bad either."

When he looked up, Sammy was gone. "I wish he'd stop doing that," Ryan thought to himself. He picked up the phone and called Lisa, his new Lab Manager.

Chapter V: A New Way of Doing Things

When Lisa picked up the phone, Ryan asked if she had time to come to his office to visit for a little while.

Lisa said, "Why, what did I do wrong now, Mr. Michaels?"

Ryan laughed. "Lisa, you didn't do anything wrong. I just want to talk with you to see how you are doing."

Somewhat hesitantly, Lisa said, "Uhh, OK. I'll be right down."

As Lisa was walking to Mr. Michaels' office, she felt nervous. She was brand new in her management position – less than two months – and this was the first time Mr. Michaels had called her to his office. She knew she was in trouble, or he wouldn't want to see her. She thought to herself, I wonder what I did? I suppose it could be about when I yelled at that new girl I hired. But she deserved it! She's supposed to know how to draw blood without hurting the patient, and the way that patient complained, I know the new girl hurt her. Twice. That's the only thing Lisa could think of as she walked toward his office. In any case, she was in trouble. Why else would he want to see me, she thought. Alone, in his office, and not a managers meeting. Yup, she was going to be fired. She knew it!

Lisa approached Mr. Michaels' outer office and Ryan's Administrative Assistant, Donna, saw her. She buzzed Ryan to let him know Lisa was there. Lisa could hear him say for her to come right in.

Uh-oh, she thought.

Lisa walked into his office and just stood there somewhat awkwardly. Ryan looked up from what he was doing and said, "Hi Lisa, have a seat."

Lisa started right in. "This is about the new girl isn't it? She deserved to be yelled at, Mr. Michaels. We're supposed to be all about patient care, customer service and creating a total customer experience, and she caused that patient pain. She deserved it!"

Ryan looked surprised. This was the first he had heard about any problems down in Lab. "What happened?" he asked.

"Well," Lisa started, "She had a problem finding a good vein to draw the patient's blood and when she did, I heard the patient go 'ouch!' So she tried another vein and the same thing happened. When she started to try a third time, I stopped her and did it myself. After the patient left, I let her have it. Like I said, she deserved it!"

Ryan looked concerned. "Did she know about our policy on draws?"

"Which one is that?" Lisa looked confused.

"Lisa, you know which one. The policy that says that after two draws, the technician is supposed to find a co-worker and have them do it. That's what policy."

Lisa could feel her face flush. "Actually, Mr. Michaels, I didn't know I was supposed to actually go over the policies with her. I just assumed she would know. I gave her the policy manual for

Lab and told her to read it, but I didn't actually ask her if she did or if she had any questions."

Ryan smiled at her and said, "Lisa, first lesson in leadership. Never assume anything when it comes to new staff, or for that matter, any of your staff. You should be talking with them about their job and making sure they have everything they need to be successful in their job. That's the only way, ultimately, that they will improve. It's your job to make sure that you set them up to be successful. Sounds like you set her up to fail, this time."

You should practice what you preach, Lisa thought to herself.

"Lisa, did you apologize to the patient?"

"No, I forgot to, Mr. Michaels."

"The first thing I'd like you to do when you get back to your office, Lisa, is call that patient up and apologize. Then write her a note apologizing again. Our patient satisfaction surveys are bad enough without having another upset patient."

"You know, Mr. Michaels, I have a sister who is a nurse at a hospital in Florida. We were talking about customer service when she came to stay with us over Christmas last year. She was saying that since her hospital wrote service standards for all of the direct-contact departments, their satisfaction scores went way up. It took a while, but their CEO was real supportive and got behind it. It started to be really successful."

Ryan wasn't a big fan of customer service standards – especially scripted ones. My staff is smart, he thought. They know that customer service is important. They know enough to be nice, but he wanted to appear interested, so he said, "How long did it take them to start seeing positive results?"

"Two years," Lisa said.

"Two years?" Ryan couldn't believe it. "Two years seems like a long time for our patients to start noticing customer service improvement."

"Yeah, I thought so too, Mr. Michaels. But my sister explained that it took some of the staff a while to get on board. Some of the long-time staff didn't think it was necessary. They thought that good customer service was just common sense. It was kind of funny. She called them historians, because they always remembered how things used to be, and it used to be that people were more polite, they said. But once they saw that their CEO was really passionate about it, they started to change. Once the CEO told them why it was so important to think of new ways, new ideas to improve customer service, they listened." Lisa continued. "What he did was pretty neat. He got all staff involved. Actively solicited ideas from everyone. Once that happened, and once everyone understood how important it was to the success of the hospital, just about everyone got on board."

Ryan was listening now. What that CEO did was explain to everyone why the standards were such worthwhile work, he thought. "Well", Ryan said, "it's certainly something to consider, but that's a conversation for another day. Let's talk about the reason I called you in here in the first place."

Here it comes, thought Lisa. "And exactly why is that, Mr. Michaels?"

Ryan decided to take a page right out of Dr. Blanchard's book. "I wanted to know how everything is going in your new position? I know you're new to a leadership position, and I wanted to make sure everything is going OK. Is there anything you need from me to be a better manager?"

Lisa felt a bit more comfortable now that she knew she wasn't in trouble, so she said, "Mr. Michaels, before, you mentioned something about me setting the new girl up to fail. Isn't that what you did to me?"

Ryan could feel the blood rising to his head, but he took a deep breath. "What do you mean, I set you up to fail?"

All of a sudden Lisa felt nervous again. Maybe she shouldn't have said that. Well, it was too late now, she thought. "Don't get me wrong, Mr. Michaels. It was very flattering when you promoted me to Lab Manager. I know you told me that it was because I was doing such an outstanding job as a Tech, and that I got along so well with everyone that you thought I would make an excellent manager. The only problem was that I have never managed people before, and no one told me what I was supposed to do. I didn't have a clue." There, she finally said it, she thought.

Ryan took a deep breath. She was right and he knew it. Sammy had warned him, in a way. "You know, Lisa, you're right. I haven't been a very good boss lately and that's about to change. I am going to start a new way of doing things with you and the rest of the managers. Starting with you, I am going to meet individually with each of the managers to see how they are doing and what they need from me to do a more effective job – to be a more effective boss. I guess I just assumed everything would be OK, and I shouldn't have done that."

He stopped for a second and then continued. "A friend of mine and I have been talking a great deal lately about leadership, and he pointed out to me that one of our jobs as leaders is to be responsive to the needs of our employees so that they can become completely responsible for their jobs. I haven't been doing that, Lisa, and I'm sorry. I have been setting you up to fail as a manager. Who knows, I probably have been setting all of the managers up to fail. We're going to change that."

Lisa couldn't believe what she was hearing. She had been thinking the same thing since Mr. Michaels had made her a manager. She didn't know the first thing about managing people and she was scared. A lot of the people she was managing were friends of hers and they expected special treatment – especially when she was doing the weekend scheduling. She had wished someone would give her some leadership training, or at least someone to mentor her. Now was her chance.

"I'm so glad to hear you say that, Mr. Michaels. I guess I never really looked at it like that, but we really do need to be responsive and support the people we manage, so that they can become better at their jobs. I didn't really know what to do with the new girl, so I yelled at her. That was the first thing that came to my mind. Maybe if I had trained her better and communicated our policies and procedures, it would have turned out differently. That friend of yours really knows what he is talking about."

Ryan just smiled. "His name is Sammy."

"Do you think I could meet him?" Lisa was anxious to learn more.

"Well," Ryan said, "I'm not sure. He seems to show up unannounced most of the time. I never really know when he's going to be here. But the next time I see him, I'll see if I can work it out. For right now, though, what exactly do you need from me to get more comfortable with your position, Lisa."

Lisa didn't hesitate. "Mr. Michaels, I need leadership training, or a mentor, or something! I don't know the first thing about how to lead and motivate my staff. I just thought they could motivate themselves, but that isn't working. I've talked to some of the other managers, and I know they feel the same way too."

Ryan was shocked. He didn't realize that his managers were that much in the dark when it came to being leaders of their departments. He simply said, "I had no idea, Lisa."

Somewhat uneasily, Lisa said, "Most of the managers are afraid of you, Mr. Michaels."

"What!"

"Don't get me wrong, Mr. Michaels. They're not afraid of you in that way. They just know that you have your own way of doing things, and when you tell them to do it a certain way, they better do it that way or you get a little upset. It's not that everyone feels that your way is necessarily wrong; it's just that there usually is more than one way to accomplish a task, and we'd like the chance sometimes to do it our way. To be honest, sometimes it feels like we check our brains at the door when we come to work and we're your little robots."

Ryan was stunned. None of his managers had ever talked to him this way before. For a second he felt hopeless. He said nothing.

Oh no, Lisa thought. Now she really had gone too far. I wish he would say something. Anything.

Finally, he said, "Thank you, Lisa. No one has ever told me that before, and I appreciate it. Sometimes I get wrapped up in my own little world, and I forget about the important things. It's the staff that will make this hospital successful, but that only can happen if the bosses do their jobs. And I guess it all starts with me. We will address this at our next managers meeting, and start the ball rolling. We are going to start to do things a little differently around here, beginning with the way I communicate with you and the rest of the managers. I'm so sorry, Lisa. And thank you so much for making me aware."

Lisa was relieved, to say the least. "That's all right, Mr. Michaels. It's not too late – at least for me. I'm brand new. You know, it's the first time I've really felt comfortable talking to you. I just didn't think that you cared about my opinion that much. Thanks for listening."

She didn't have to add that, Ryan thought. Of course he cared about what his managers thought. I guess I'd better start listening a little bit more. Starting with the managers meeting.

****

After his conversation with Lisa, Ryan called a managers meeting for a few days later. When Ann, the Director of Nursing, received the email referencing the special managers meeting, she couldn't help but think that Mr. Michaels had too many meetings and until recently, they hadn't been very productive. Usually, she thought, the meetings only consisted of Mr. Michaels talking about his agendas - what had to be done and when. Nothing about why we were doing it. Mostly, she thought, Mr. Michaels just liked to hear himself talk.

As the managers filed in for the special meeting, there was a lot of mumbling. Things like: "here we go again, what's this meeting about?" and "it seems like all we ever do is go to meetings."

When Ryan entered the conference room, he sat down, took a deep breath and started in.

"Thank you all for taking the time for what I think is a very important conversation." Many of the managers just rolled their eyes. He always said that.

Ryan continued. "I have been having some fairly in-depth conversations with a special new friend of mine about leadership. He pointed out to me that I may not be leading you all the best way that I could and that I may be actually setting many of you up to fail. If that is true, I apologize. If that is true, things are going to change around here beginning with the way that I communicate with you – individually and as a leadership team."

Ann looked at Linda, the Housekeeping Manager. They both looked shocked. Mr. Michaels never apologizes, Ann thought. This must be some kind of new friend that he has.

The managers were really listening now as Ryan continued. " I had a conversation with Lisa the other day and she really opened my eyes. In the next few weeks, I will meet with each of you individually to help you assess your departmental improvement, challenges, and help you make a plan to become a better manager. I think these conversations will help us all become better managers. I want all of you to be completely successful with your own teams, and I haven't done a very good job of giving you the tools and resources that you need to become winners, so to speak. Lisa told me that many of you would appreciate it if you had an opportunity for leadership development. Is that true?"

Most of the managers just looked at each other, not really feeling comfortable saying anything.

Ryan said, "Look, I want you all to feel comfortable saying anything you want to me, especially if you think that I may be making a mistake."

Wow, Jim thought. Jim, the Maintenance Manager, had never really felt comfortable around Mr. Michaels. He spoke up anyway. "Mr. Michaels, I think I can speak for most of us. We have talked about this before, and yes, I think most all of us need some leadership training – or development, as you call it. Most of us were promoted through the ranks and have had to learn about leading our staff almost by trial and error. I think I am very good at the technical aspects of my job, but I know that I have a hard time developing and motivating my own staff. I know that many of the other managers feel the same way."

"OK then," Ryan said, "does anyone know someone or a company who does leadership training?"

Everyone was silent. No one knew anything about leadership development or who to contact.

"Well," Ryan said, "I think my new friend will have an idea or two. In fact, I'm sure he will. As soon as I see him, I will ask him and get it set up. In the mean time, starting tomorrow, I will make appointments with each of you to discuss the things you need from me to do your job more effectively. Thanks again for taking the time. Meeting adjourned."

The managers just looked at each other. This had to be the shortest meeting on record – 20 minutes. As they filed out of the conference room, Linda walked up next to Lisa and whispered, "You're my new hero. How did you ever have the nerve to tell Mr. Michaels those things? Great job!"

"It wasn't easy," Lisa said. "Actually, when he called me in his office I thought I was in big trouble. When he told me what he wanted, I was completely shocked. I really think he's trying to change. His new friend – I think his name is Sammy – must have really had an impact on him. I would love to have the opportunity to meet this guy."

Lisa didn't know, but she would never have that opportunity.

Chapter VI: "Sten?"

Over the next several weeks, Ryan had met with most of his managers, and his eyes were opened. Not only was he leading many of them wrongly, he discovered that when he actually listened to them, they had some very good ideas. He started becoming much more collaborative in his thinking and depending on the manager, started the process of leading them in much more effective ways. He started giving them the "tools and resources" they needed to do their job better. They seemed to be a little cautious at the start of the meetings, but once he made them feel more comfortable, the floodgates opened. They started blasting him – in a positive way, if that was possible – for his past methods, and thanked him for being willing to change and listen to them.

Ryan felt some positive changes in his managers' attitude and work ethic, but not completely. They had all asked about the leadership training and he hadn't done anything yet. He was waiting for Sammy to show up again. Where was he, Ryan thought. It had been almost two months since Sammy was here the last time. Maybe he wasn't coming back anymore. Maybe he thought his work was done here, and Ryan was supposed to do the rest on his own. I suppose, Ryan thought, that I could contact the State Hospital Association and get a trainer's name from them. He'd give Sammy one more week, he thought, and if he didn't show up by then, he contact the Association.

As Ryan was walking down the hallway to his office, he met Lisa. Lisa smiled and said hello and stopped. "Mr. Michaels, I just wanted to thank you for following through on what you said you would do. All of the managers I have talked to are really excited about your new approach with them. We all are inspired to be able to do the same things with our staff. When are we going to have the leadership training?"

Ryan sighed. "I am working on it, Lisa. I'll have an answer for everyone in a week or so. And thanks again for opening my eyes."

Lisa just beamed.

Ryan walked in to his outer office, said hello to Donna, walked into his office and shut the door.

And there he was.

Sammy was sitting in the chair across from Ryan's desk with his feet propped up on it. He was humming some song Ryan vaguely recognized. Some oldie out of the sixties, Ryan thought.

Ryan smiled. He was glad to see him. "As rude as you are just showing up like this, I'm really glad to see you Sammy!"

"So," Sammy smiled, "you had a meeting with your managers, and then started the process of meeting individually with them. Things going a little better, Ryan?"

"How did you know that?" Ryan had to admit that he was continually surprised at how Sammy knew exactly what was going on.

Sammy started scratching his left arm as he sat there. "I have my contacts, Ryan. I told you that before. Now that the process has started, your managers are itching for some leadership training, aren't they?"

"You are amazing, Sammy. Yes, you're right. They are. Can you do the training, or do you know someone who can?"

As Sammy continued to scratch his arm, he said "Sten."

"Sten?" Ryan asked. "What is a Sten?"

"It's not a what, it's a who," Sammy said. "His name is Sten Markson, simply the best trainer for leadership around. I use him frequently."

Ryan cocked his head to the side a little. "You mean Stan, don't you?"

Now Sammy was vigorously scratching his arm. "No, his name is Sten. He's a little strange, just like his name. However, he is very, very good."

"I suppose he's one of your golfing buddies," Ryan asked.

"Actually, he doesn't play golf. He plays tennis and is quite good. But no golf." Sammy was shaking his head. "I told you he was a little strange. Actually, I used to go to Vegas with him and his tennis buddies, but I ended up playing golf by myself while they played tennis. Guess I got too lonesome, so I stopped going."

Ryan was smiling. "That's too bad, Sammy, but if he doesn't play golf, I like him already. How do I contact him?"

Still scratching, Sammy said, "I'll take care of it. I'll let him know you're interested and he will contact you."

"Thanks Sammy. I appreciate it. A lot! What's wrong with your arm? You've been scratching it since you've been here. Got a rash?"

Sammy really looked sheepish. "It's the darn patch. It's driving me crazy!"

"Patch?" Ryan looked surprised.

"No lectures, OK? And don't judge me." Sammy was really upset. "The gum didn't work, the suckers didn't work. So I'm trying the patch, OK?"

Ryan burst out laughing. "Getting a bit touchy, aren't you?"

"Ryan, it's the toughest thing I've ever tried to do. You don't know how many times that I have cursed you for making me do this!"

Ryan looked concerned. He opened his desk to find something and as he was looking, said, "Sammy, it's for your own good. You know as well as I do that smoking is dangerous to yourself and others. It takes a lot of willpower and commitment. I should know. I used to smoke two packs a day. Finally, one day when I woke up hacking, I just said 'That's it'! I quit cold turkey. It was really tough, but I had a plan and stuck to it. For someone who talks a lot about commitment and planning, you seem to have a pretty difficult time practicing what you preach. Here it is. I knew I had some information on a Quit Smoking Clinic. So…when is this Sten guy going to contact me about some leadership development for my staff?"

When Ryan looked up, Sammy wasn't there anymore, but Ryan thought he could still hear him scratching. What was the deal with this guy, Ryan thought. Every time I have something important to ask him, he disappears. Could he possibly be just a figment of my imagination, he thought? Impossible! He wasn't that crazy!

****

Over the next weeks, Ryan continued to have his conversations with his managers. He could tell that they all started to feel a bit more comfortable talking with him – telling him what was on their minds. They talked about the improvement of processes within their own department. They talked about the ideas and personal visions that they had to improve. They talked about how Ryan could give them the proper tools and resources necessary to do better.

Ryan discovered as time went on that they started to trust him. They started to open up about their fears of not getting things exactly right. Ryan continually assured them that running a department is not only a tough job, but it is a learning process. He encouraged all of them to start involving their own team in sharing improvement ideas.

He thought he noticed a new desire – a new drive – with some of the staff. They were actually talking about how they could all do a better job, and talking about those two incredibly important words – worthwhile work.

But Ryan was still troubled. Almost daily, at least one of his managers asked him about when they were going to start their leadership training, and Ryan didn't have an answer for them. He hadn't seen or heard from Sammy in almost six weeks, and this Sten guy hadn't called like Sammy had promised he would. He really hoped that Sammy would show up soon or the momentum he had gained over the past months would be lost. The managers were finally eager for education, and Ryan wasn't producing.

When Ryan walked in to his office the next morning, there was a voice mail for him. It was Sten, asking Ryan to call him as soon as possible.

Ryan was excited when he listened to the message, and he phoned Sten immediately.

After a few rings, the man answered: "Markson Management Consulting, this is Sten."

"Sten, this is Ryan Michaels returning your call. I'm so glad that you finally contacted me."

"I apologize for not contacting you earlier, Ryan, but I have been swamped. I travel a lot and this really is the first opportunity I've had. My friend Sammy mentioned that you might be interested in some leadership training."

"Absolutely," Ryan said. All of my managers are quite eager to start. Sammy said you were really good."

Sten laughed a little. "That's very kind of Sammy. He and I go way back, and he has thrown a lot of work my way."

"Sten, can you tell me a little more about Sammy and his background. He is one strange man! He seems to show up in my office at the most unexpected times. He seems very knowledgeable, but keeps his background pretty private – and he always has a new gimmick to quit smoking."

Sten roared. "Sammy has been trying to quit smoking ever since I've known him. He just can't seem to get over the hump. As far as his background, I really can't tell you much. I know he's very successful in turning organizational leadership around. I met him several years ago at one of my workshops. He actually wasn't at the workshop itself, but showed up right after one of them in Denver. We started talking and he said that he had been following my career and that he thought that I was one of the best leadership trainers he had ever seen. He asked if he could use me as a resource for training in the future because he wasn't able to actually do the training himself. I said that he could."

What Ryan didn't know was that Sten wasn't completely truthful about what he said.

Ryan was curious. "Did he ever say why he couldn't do the training himself?"

Sten was quiet for a long time and then said, "No, I guess he never really did explain that. He used to go to Vegas with my friends and me, but stopped going a few years back."

"Yeah," Ryan said. "He mentioned that."

"That was another strange thing about Sammy," Sten abruptly said. "He would never actually travel with us to Vegas. We would always have to meet him there. At the hotel. Great blackjack player, though. He always seemed to know when the good cards would start coming. In all of the years we were in Vegas together, I never once saw him lose money. Strangest thing. Amazing guy."

"Getting back on track," Ryan started, "I would really like for you to do some leadership training for us."

"You would, or you and your managers would?"

A bit startled at the question, Ryan said, "Well, of course my managers and I both would. They have been pestering me for weeks and weeks about it."

"Then great!" Sten said. "When did you have in mind to do this?"

"As soon as possible," Ryan said. "In the next 30 days, if possible."

"30 days!" Sten said almost yelling. "Are you kidding me? I work at least six months out. The soonest I could do it is next June."

"Next June? But this is only November. We'll lose all of the momentum I've established in the last two months. Next June? You must be joking! Please! We have to do it before next June." Ryan was panicking.

Silence again at the other end. Then, "Well Ryan, since Sammy seems to have taken you on as a project, I guess I do owe him a favor or two. Let me see what I can do and I'll call you back in the next hour. Will you be in your office?"

"Yes, I will wait here for your call, Sten. Please, do what you can." Ryan seemed a little more relieved.

After he hung up, Ryan's thoughts turned back to Sammy. His friend Sten didn't seem to know a whole lot about Sammy either.

Just then Ann, the Director of Nursing, appeared at the entrance to his office. "Any more on the leadership training?" she asked.

Ryan smiled. "Great timing Ann. I just got off the phone with one of the best leadership trainers in the country, according to my friend. He's going to call me back this morning to set a date."

"That would be great," Ann said. "I have some issues in my department that I really need help with."

"What kind of issues?"

"Well," Ann started, "two different kinds. One is about one of my staff's attitude, and with another, it's about improving her skills. I'm really not too sure what to do about either of them. They're both friends of mine on top of everything else."

"There's always something, isn't there Ann? We will talk about this later, if you want, but let's wait first to see how fast we can get this leadership training scheduled."

"Thanks a lot Mr. Michaels. You should know that I am finding it much easier to come to you lately. I've really noticed a change. And so have the other managers. Whoever this new friend of yours is, he has really helped you. Our communication seems to be so much better. "

Ryan smiled. "Thanks Ann."

"That's all right. I just thought you should know how much we all appreciate it."

Just then the phone rang. Ryan motioned for Ann to sit down, but he had to take the call.

"This is Ryan Michaels. How may I help you?"

"Hey Ryan, this is Sten."

"That was quick," Ryan said somewhat surprised that he was calling back so soon.

"I told you I would see what I could do, and one of the first clients I called back was willing to change dates. How does three weeks from tomorrow sound to you?"

Ryan was absolutely, but pleasantly shocked. "Great!" Ryan was almost shouting. He gave a thumbs up to Ann. "I appreciate this so much, Sten."

It took them about fifteen minutes to work out the details, and Ann was patiently waiting for Ryan to get finished with the call. She could tell from the way the conversation was going that they were discussing the details of a leadership workshop. She was excited.

After Ryan hung up, he was beaming. "Great news, Ann. We will be able to have the leadership training in three weeks, so we have to get some quick planning done. The workshop will be mandatory for all managers, and it will take up two full days. I know you have a lot of experience in planning and scheduling events, so would you be willing to put this together for us?"

"I would love to," Ann said excitedly. "And I don't think you have to worry about the mandatory part of it. All of us have been asking for this for a long time."

After Ryan and Ann finished going over the details, Ann was getting ready to leave and turned to Ryan and said, "Thank you so much, Mr. Michaels. Wait 'til I tell the others. They'll be so excited."

"Thank you, Ann. I really appreciate your dedication and passion on this. Keep me informed."

Chapter VII: Finally, Leadership Development

Over the next few weeks, Ann and Donna, Ryan's Administrative Assistant, met several times on the details of Sten's upcoming workshop. They made sure all of the managers cleared their schedule and checked with Sten more than a few times to make sure they had everything he needed – all of the audio and visual needs. They also looked for an appropriate location off-site to hold the workshop. Sten said that it was very important to get them away from the hospital. He said that having it at the hospital offered too many temptations for the managers to go back to their office and check on things during the breaks. He would have none of that. He also asked Donna to put a memo out to all managers to keep their cell phones off while the workshop was in session.

Cell phones were one of Sten's pet peeves. He would be right in the middle of making a point, and someone's cell phone would go off. It made him crazy! Finally, in one of his workshops, he made an announcement at the beginning. He said if anyone's phone rang during the presentation, he would take it away. He made sure everyone understood. Sure enough over the course of any one of his workshops, he would collect one or two. He always gave them back at the end of the day – but not before. The word got around about this, and slowly but surely, he had no more problems.

Donna and Ann finally found a location away from the hospital. They made arrangements to hold the workshop in one of the banquet rooms at the Mecca Casino and Resort about 50 miles away. It was a large enough room and they would take care of the catering of the continental breakfast for both days and sandwiches for lunch on the first day. It was expensive, but they both thought it was worth it. They thought it was important to make this special.

Finally, all of the arrangements were made, and they went to Ryan to inform him of the details and to get his final approval.

Ryan did a bit of a double-take when he was told of the cost, but he also thought the time should be special and it was worth the extra expense.

"Thank you both very much," Ryan said appreciatively. "You both did a great job. I had no doubt that you could handle the details and besides that, you took a great deal of pressure off me. I really appreciate it. Now, is there anything I can do for you, or do you have it all taken care of?"

They both smiled, and Ann said, "I think we have it all done Mr. Michaels. I just really want to thank you for making this happen."

Ryan smiled broadly. He had to admit, he was excited, too. There was no question in his mind that he also needed the leadership training.

****

The day was finally here. All of the managers – every one of them- were gathered in the meeting room at the Mecca Casino. So was Ryan Michaels. Everyone seemed so excited, Ryan thought. He was pleased.

Everything was set up. The PowerPoint showed a "Welcome Bedford Community Hospital" on the screen. All of the materials were placed at the tables, along with named table tents for each of the managers and Ryan. Coffee, rolls and water were available for all, but it was fifteen minutes before the session was supposed to start and one thing was missing. Sten.

About ten minutes before it was to start, an older man walked in. He appeared to be in his late '60s at least. He was tall and thin. He had very thick white hair that was combed mostly straight back.

This man walked right up to Ryan and said with a broad smile, "You must be Ryan Michaels. Sammy described you perfectly. I'm Sten Markson. Glad to meet you. Let's get started and I can talk with you more during lunch today. Man, I'm already hungry!"

Somewhat startled, Ryan quickly stood up and shook Sten's hand and introduced himself. Ryan thought he grimaced a little when Sten shook his hand – he had the strongest grip he had felt in a long, long time. What a character, Ryan thought. And what's the deal with the white hair? Everyone he had met lately had white hair. At least this guy cut his hair, Ryan thought, referring to Sammy's long hair and ponytail.

Sten walked to the front of the room and looked around at everyone. Suddenly, all of the talking stopped and all of the managers focused their eyes on Sten. They all were thinking the same thing; This must be the guy. Standing in front of us is, according to all of the information we have, one of the leading experts on leadership in the country. They were in awe.

Even Ryan was a little mesmerized. Suddenly, he felt like a good boss. These people want to be here, he thought. I should have done this a long time ago. But then he started thinking that Sten looked a little long in the tooth to be doing a day-and-a-half workshop. He better be good. He sure as heck charges enough. I hope he's worth it.

He didn't know it yet, but Ryan was in for the best training experience of his life.

****

Sten was ready to start. He smiled broadly at everyone, briskly rubbed his hand together, and said, "Let's get started. My name is Sten Markson, and it is so good to be with you all at the Mecca. It's the first time I have been in this area, and it is beautiful. Thank you so much for having me."

He continued. "But that's not why we are here. We're not here to talk about how beautiful everything is, or even how good it is to be here. We are here to start your journey. Today, we are all getting on the bus and we're starting the longest journey of our lives – the journey to becoming an effective leader. The final destination? There is none. Effective leadership is a journey, not a destination. Along this journey, we will gather knowledge and experience rather than souvenirs. We will go on this journey together, helping each other, not going it alone. Because always remember, none of us is as smart as all of us."

Sten started walking around the room. He was looking at everyone, gazing into their eyes. He could tell he had their attention. That's one thing he could always do. Keep their attention.

Sten kept pacing, but then he stopped right in front of Linda, the Housekeeping Manager and looked right at her. "That's why I think we are all here" he said. "But I need to hear from each of you why you are here. So I'm going to go around the tables and ask each of you two questions: Why are you here? and What are some of the key things you want to learn in the next few days? Linda, let's start with you."

Sten went around the tables and asked everyone the same questions and for the most part, they were the typical answers that he had heard before:

Linda said she wanted to learn how to be more effective managing her staff.

Ann said she wanted to learn how she could motivate her staff better.

Jim from Maintenance said he wanted to learn how to manage his staff and still get his work done.

But when Sten got to Ryan, it was a different answer than he had heard before. Ryan said, "Well Sten, I really want to become a more passionate leader and instill that same passion in my managers."

"Aha!" Sten said. "You hit on the real secret of learning to become a more effective leader. Passion. Passion for the vision of your hospital. Passion for the goals. Passion for what you do, knowing that what you do is so worthwhile. Tell me – anyone – what is the biggest spectator sport in this country?"

They all had different answers: Pro football, basketball, soccer, NASCAR racing. Sten had heard them all before.

Sten just blurted it out. "Boss watching! Boss watching is without question the biggest spectator sport in this country!"

They all laughed, but he continued. "I'm serious. Think about it. When your staff goes on break, goes out for a beer after work, or just get together at someone's house, what invariably will come up? Work! And within that context, who will they talk about? Their boss."

He continued. "And just what are they saying about you? Are they talking about how much enthusiasm – how much passion – you have for your work? Or are they saying that you look like you really don't care? The point is, if you expect to instill passion, enthusiasm, excitement and positive attitudes in your staff, it all starts with you."

"You see, they will model your behavior. And if you can consistently show that passion - that excitement – some of it will rub off on your staff and make your job that much easier. What you do is important. As a matter of fact, it's critical. It's all right to show your enthusiasm. Get excited. Show your staff how passionate you are. I guarantee you it will be worth it."

Sten knew he was on a roll now, and the workshop really hadn't even begun yet, so he continued. "Now don't get me wrong. We are human. We don't always have those up days and aren't always that excited about going to work in the morning. And that, ladies and gentlemen, is what makes our job so tough. As leaders, we have to visibly display that excitement, that passion, that positive attitude every day – whether we really feel that way or not; because, you see, they are watching us. Every day! And besides that, you're the boss! So what do you say, let's get started."

****

Over the next day and a half, they talked about a lot of leadership tools and methods. They discussed Situational Leadership II and the concept that you must lead each of your staff according to their abilities and motivation on any one particular task. They talked about the process of discovering what those abilities and motivations were –"diagnosing" their development level, Sten called it. He said that they could not just assume where they were on any one task based on prior performance of a different task. Sten said that's where many managers fail. They assume. They don't take the time to sit down with each of their staff and discuss their jobs, their goals and ask them – using what Sten called "common language" about their abilities and motivation and passion to do the job. Then, with that information, they can understand how they have to lead them.

It made sense to all of the managers, and to Ryan – and it was something they could put to use immediately. Ryan also noticed that Sten seemed to have injured his arm. Every so often, Sten would grab his arm like it was hurting him, and then start scratching. He thought about Sammy.

They had exercises, role plays, and even played a few leadership games. Ryan was extremely impressed with this guy.

Sten spent quite a bit of time talking about the goals of each department. He asked for a raise of hands on how many managers had goals for their department. Only six of them raised their hand. He said that without goals, departments will ultimately not improve the way they should, and that they would "wallow in the depths of mediocrity."

"Goals," Sten said, "are the lifeblood of every organization – of every department. They are essential if we are serious about taking Bedford Community Hospital to another level. They are essential to continuous improvement. And they can be motivating for some of your staff – certainly not all of them, because different things motivate different people. It is our job to find out what motivates each of our staff, but for some of them, goals are a tool you can use."

Sten talked about how everyone had probably heard about SMART goals – the acronym for Specific, Measurable, Attainable, Relevant, and Timebound or something similar. But he said he had a different acronym for what a great goal should be – DIRECT.

He wrote DIRECT on the flipchart, and under it wrote the following:

Demanding
In sync (with the hospital's strategic goals)
Responsible
Empowering
Clear
Timely (or time-bound)

Sten went on to say that all departmental goals should be based on the strategic goals of the hospital – that they must be "in sync" with those goals – so everyone will be on the same page, working together toward the same ultimate result. He said goals must be fair, but that they also must be demanding – they must stretch the limits of everyone in the department.

He went on to say that all departmental goals have to be responsible in that they cannot be frivolous, and that they must be empowering to the staff so that they will take ownership in the results. Goals, he said, must be clear. Everyone has to understand exactly what we are doing, how we will do it and why they are so important to the success of our hospital – the worthwhile work in them. The very best performance, Sten said, starts with clear goals.

And finally, Sten said that the goals must be timely to what is going on in our hospital, and that they must have a deadline – whether that deadline is two weeks, two months or two years. "A goal without a deadline is just a good idea," Sten said.

Finally, Sten said that the entire Management Team should sit down together and make a plan for the next year on what the strategic goals of the hospital should be, and then, based on those strategic goals, work together on what the departmental goals should be. He said that is necessary because many of the departmental goals will affect other departments, so why not work on those goals together. Doing it that way, Sten said, will help us become a better and more effective Management Team. It is teamwork in its purest form, he said.

"And that, ladies and gentlemen, will make your job easier working to construct a better team within your own department, because when your staff sees all of you working better together, it will give them the incentive to look within their own department to model that same behavior.....And they are watching, you know. Because what is one of their favorite pastimes?" Sten asked.

"Boss Watching!" everyone said and started to laugh.

One of the other things Sten discussed in his workshop was effective recognition. He said that no one does it enough. No one takes the time because they don't think they have it.

"How long does it take to say 'thank you'? Two seconds? We must take the time because it's that important. Think about the last time you did something great and no one said anything. How did it make you feel?" Everyone nodded like they all remembered when it happened. Sten continued. "It made you feel pretty rotten, didn't it? Like no one noticed, no one cared. Do you think for one minute that any of your staff feels any different when that happens to them? Sometimes we have to look for it, watch them to catch them doing things well, but watch what happens when we start noticing those things. That good work will start happening more often. Attitudes will change. Morale will improve, and they'll start recognizing each other. It will become a culture of gratitude – an attitude of gratitude."

Sten knew he had their complete attention, so he continued. "As I said before, we mean well, we mean to recognize our staff, and some of us do. We just don't do it enough. I have never been in a hospital, or a hospital department where there has been a sign that said: 'Stop recognizing me – There's way too much of that going on here!'"

Everyone laughed, but they got the point. Sten started scratching again.

"One last thing on recognition," Sten said. "We all have to make effective recognition part of our daily to-do list. Effective recognition must be right at the top of that list every day. And if you don't have a daily to-do list, start tomorrow. Remember, you will get what you recognize."

Sten also talked about departmental celebrations. "Be a celebrations manager," he said. "Celebrations don't even have to be about anything. Celebrate because it's Tuesday! But for sure, celebrate the important thing like goal completion, birthdays, improved customer surveys and welcoming new team members. Use your imagination! If you don't have one, find one." He was teasing them now. "Celebrations are motivating for many people, and they are necessary for us because we all work in a very stressful environment. Celebrations will ease that stress, if even for just a few minutes. Celebrations can re-energize your staff. Take the time. If you do, those celebrations may reap huge morale boosts for your staff and for yourself."

"And finally," Sten said looking clearly at Ryan, "hire the good people. Hire the people with smiles on their face and a shining personality. As long as they have the technical skills required, hire based on their attitude. You can train the rest. Remember the most expensive person we will ever hire is the one we have to fire."

"Remember that our job as managers is to give our people the necessary training and expectations – grow them up in their tasks, so to speak. Motivate them, congratulate them, lead them. But ultimately, we must let the people who do the work, do the work."

"Walk your talk," Sten continued. Back up your words with action, because people will ultimately believe more of what they see than what they hear. In the end, it will be your staff that brings great success to your hospital and to your department, but that can only happen through effective leadership at all levels. Thank you for having me. You have been an interested group. You have challenged me with great questions and I appreciated that. But now it's your time. It's time to start your journey. It's time to get on that bus. Remember, along the journey, you'll have a few flat tires, but just get out and fix those flats and get right back on the bus."

Sten got a standing ovation. Everyone cheered. They were excited and it showed.

Ryan had to admit, it was the best leadership development he had ever received. He was starting to pack up his materials, and Ryan noticed what he had written down on a note pad:

1. Leadership Passion.
2. Don't assume, diagnose.
3. Strategic goals – together.
4. Recognition to-do list.
5. All above focus in managers meeting.

Ryan was pumped and he wasn't about to let the managers lose their excitement and passion from the last day and a half. He was committed to having monthly discussions about what just took place, how everyone was doing with it and how each of them could improve. So many ideas were going through his mind, he could barely contain himself. He hadn't been this excited about anything since the first few years he was the CEO of his first hospital, he thought. The passion was back. This time he wouldn't lose it.

Ryan walked over to Sten and shook his hand. "Sten, that was the most amazing day and a half I have ever spent in leadership development. Best ever. I really learned a lot. Thank you so much!"

"You're welcome," Sten said with a broad smile. "I actually get that a lot. I guess I know I'm good, and I just always hope that the group that I'm training pays attention and gets it. This was a really good group."

Ryan was a little taken aback by Sten's response. Man, that guy is arrogant, Ryan thought to himself. He also thought Sten smelled a bit like cigarette smoke. Couldn't be, Ryan thought. I never once saw him smoke during the breaks. But then he thought about the times he saw Sten scratching his arm like Sammy. I wonder if he's trying to quit smoking like Sammy and is using a patch, too. His thoughts turned to Sammy. "Have you talked to Sammy lately?" Ryan asked Sten.

Sten rolled his eyes and said, "Not really. I guess I haven't spoken to him since he called me about you wanting this training. Sammy is one strange guy. I'm not sure what his story is. He seems to just pop up out of the blue, and as quick as that happens, he's gone."

"I know the feeling," Ryan said.

Ryan and Sten shook hands again. Ryan thanked him again, and they said goodbye. That would be the last time they would see each other.

Chapter VIII: "Where's Sammy?"

Over the next several months, Ryan could see his managers using the tools that were provided by Sten in that "great" workshop. Managers were meeting with each of their staff more often and it seemed like most of them were gaining some insight into how they needed to lead their staff.

It seemed to Ryan like morale was better and that the managers were empowering their staff more often. Performance in the departments, by most accounts, was improving.

The managers meetings were much more productive. They were helping each other and talking about their leadership skills. Each of them took turns discussing what was working for them and what was not. Ryan just sat back and listened and ran the meetings. He was proud of himself that he had turned the corner. He may have still ran the meetings and set the agendas, but he wasn't doing all the talking anymore.

In one of the meetings, Ann, the Director of Nursing, said, "I really think we've all come a long way in our leadership skills in the last few months. We obviously still have a lot to learn, but it's a start. But isn't it time to start talking about our goals now?"

They all looked at Ryan.

"What ARE the strategic goals of the hospital?" Ann said looking at Ryan.

Ryan could feel his face turn red. The hospital didn't have any current strategic goals, and he knew it. "I think we should do that together, like Sten suggested." Ryan said. "But that will have to wait for another meeting. Maybe next month. So why don't all of you be thinking what they should be, and I'll schedule a half-day meeting for us for next month."

Ryan didn't have a clue what he was going to do, but at least he recovered well from the question Ann asked, he thought. Where was Sammy when you really needed him, he thought.

As Ryan was thinking about that, he was somewhat shocked when he remembered that he hadn't seen Sammy now in almost six months. He must have figured his work was done here, Ryan thought. But he sure could use his advice now. Ryan sighed and thought he almost missed Sammy's intrusions.

Feeling a little sad about Sammy's absence, Ryan walked back to his office. When he opened his door, he could feel it. The goose bumps. And he was right. There sat Sammy in Ryan's chair with a huge grin on his face.

"Miss me?" Sammy said.

This time Ryan didn't get mad at Sammy or yell at him for just showing up in his office. He was actually very excited and relieved to see this strange man with the white hair and pony tail.

Ryan smiled. "Actually, I did miss you Sammy. Where have you been the last six months? I guess I just thought your work here was done and that you accomplished what you came for. But here you are, showing up again when I really need you."

Sammy burst out laughing. "Done? Are you kidding! We've really just scratched the surface of what you have to do to significantly improve BCH. You have been doing a good job since the workshop – I know that. You've all improved your leadership skills, but it's time to move on to more specifics. By the way, how did the workshop go? How did you like Sten?"

"It was amazing," Ryan said. "We all learned a lot from that guy. By the way – and this is just a gut feeling – but is Sten trying to quit smoking too? Is he wearing a patch like you are?"

Sammy just shrugged his shoulders and smiled. "Couldn't tell you."

"By the way, Sammy, is it working? Have you quit for good?"

"Still wearing the patch. Still trying," is all Sammy would say about it.

Changing the subject, Ryan said, "Sammy, as far as we've come, I'm running into a problem on something, so I'm really happy you showed up."

"Let me guess," Sammy interrupted. "Goals."

Ryan just shook his head. "I don't know how you know these things, but, yes, you are absolutely right."

"I've had a lot of experience," Sammy smiled. "Where are you stuck?"

Now it was Ryan who started smiling. "I'm not stuck, Sammy. I can't get started. I remember way back when I first met you, you asked me about a Strategic Plan, and strategic goals. You knew then that we didn't have any. But then Sten said that the

Management Team and I could put the strategic goals together on our own."

"With approval and guidance from your Board," Sammy interrupted.

"Fine," Ryan said, "I can do that, but what should the goals be?"

"That depends what is most important and relevant to your hospital, Ryan. I'm not going to set the goals for you. That's your job. I can give you some suggestions, however; then it's up to you, your Board, and your Management Team as to what direction to follow. Tell me, what do you think are the most relevant issues right now and for the next few years for your hospital to thrive and grow?"

Ryan thought for a few minutes. The silence was deafening. No one said anything, and then Ryan said, "Well, as you know, our customer service surveys have been terrible lately."

"And, " Sammy prodded.

"And customer service is really important to our hospital. We have to get better."

Sammy kept prodding. "Where do you think you should be in those patient satisfaction surveys?"

"Well, I think that there isn't any reason that we couldn't be in the 90th percentile with comparable hospitals in the hospital-wide category. We used to be, but then we lost our focus."

"Because you didn't have a goal for it," Sammy interrupted. "Well, now you do. Your first strategic goal could be for BCH to be in the 90th percentile of comparable hospitals on your patient satisfaction surveys. It's certainly very measurable, and you could continually assess your progress."

"But how would the departments achieve that? What would their role be?"

Sammy stood up and hitched up his pants. "Man, you ARE really a novice at this, aren't you? I would start with the departments that have direct contact with the customers – the patients, family, friends, visitors – you know what I mean. Start by putting customer service standards in place for all of those direct-contact departments. Have them track the customer at every interaction within their department. Look at what they are doing and saying now and what it would take to improve; to make it a better experience for the patient. I'll help you more with that tomorrow. Right now let's talk more about goals."

"You mean you're going to actually be here tomorrow, too?" Ryan asked with a broad grin."

Sammy shook his head. "Wasn't planning to, but you were right. You really need some more help. What else is important to the hospital, Ryan?"

"Money," Ryan said without hesitating.

Sammy started laughing again. "I wondered how long it would take you to figure that one out. Tell me about your financial situation here at the hospital."

Ryan started to shake his head. "It's not that we're in bad shape, Sammy. It's just that I think we could be doing a lot better. The department managers have a hard time staying within the budget. On top of that, our turnover has been higher than usual the last several months, and as you know, that's expensive too."

"That's two more goals right there," Sammy said as he was thrusting his arm into the air."

"What do you mean?" Ryan was actually enjoying this. He was learning.

"Well," Sammy said, "first of all, every department has a budget. Obviously the key is staying within the budget by mapping out a plan. So another goal would be for each department to stay at or below budget while at the same time not sacrificing or maybe actually improving patient care and service. That's the tricky part. The departments could make it a bit more interesting by having contests. Any staff that came up with a cost-saving measure that was implemented would get recognition in the form of a prize, a gift certificate and their name in your newsletter. Each department could use their own imagination as to what the reward would be, as long as there wasn't any significant expense involved. In other words, it would have to be budgeted for."

Sammy continued. "And make staff turnover a goal. Set a maximum percentage that would be an improvement for the hospital on staff turnover and let the departments figure out a plan for their role in that goal. One of the key elements for the departments to remember once they have a goal is the process involved in successfully accomplishing that goal. It's all about processes, Ryan. Each goal has to have a step-by-step plan in place to accomplish that goal. Once you have that plan in place, then each manager can assign individual goals within that plan to each staff member. You have to keep the staff involved, Ryan. They need to take ownership in the goals. It will keep some of them motivated. It'll give some of them a reason for getting up and going to work each day. Make sense?"

Ryan was nodding his head. "Yes, it does, Sammy. It makes a lot of sense. So does making each department's quality of work a goal...and from that goal, quality of work goals for each staff member within that department. I think I'm getting the hang of it now. The Management Team and I, with the input and support of the Board, will provide the big picture with the hospital's strategic goals, and then each department will establish goals within the context of the strategic goals. Right?"

"Bingo!" Sammy had a huge smile on his face. ""You've got it! And the great thing is that all of these goals will provide basis for your performance evaluations which, by the way, you're going to redo after you have the goals in place."

Ryan was startled. "We are?"

"Yes, you are." Sammy had his arms folded and it sounded more like an order than a statement. "Gotta go now. Got nothing else for you today. See you tomorrow."

Just then Ryan's phone rang. As he reached to get it, he said, "But Sammy, wait a second. I have some questions on the service standards you were talking about."

But it was too late. Like every time before, Sammy was already gone.

Chapter IX: Customer Service, Sammy-Style:

The next morning, Ryan almost skipped in to work. He was really excited about the conversation he had yesterday with Sammy about goals. He thought he had some great ideas now and thought he was fully prepared for the meeting with the Board and then the meeting with his Management Team. Everything Sammy had said about the importance of goals was true. He knew he had to get the ball rolling, and he new it would help him in his quest to improve the hospital. Besides that, he thought, he had to do better for the hospital if he was going to keep his job.

When he walked into his office at 6:45a.m., there sat Sammy. Ryan was not a bit surprised that Sammy beat him to the office.

"Let's get started," Sammy said as he was scratching his arm again.

"Wait a minute, Sammy," Ryan said, just a little bit irritated. "I need to get some coffee before we start. Want some?"

"No thanks, Ryan. I don't drink the stuff. Too addictive. You know Ryan, you should really think about cutting back on the caffeine. It's not very good for you."

Ryan just glared at him. "Addictive, Sammy? I would be careful about what you think is addictive or not. Think about it."

Sammy just smiled and said, "Yeh, yeh, yeh, I know."

When Ryan came back with his coffee, he looked at Sammy and said, "OK, let's talk about service standards. Exactly what are we talking about here?"

"Well," Sammy started, "I really like to get the entire department involved. The standards have to be theirs. The managers just need to find a way to get them to stretch, to use their imaginations. After all, what we're trying to do here is go beyond our customer's expectations – continuously and consistently. That's why we have standards. But always remember, Ryan, once the standards are developed, they shouldn't remain static."

"Go on," Ryan said, paying close attention to what Sammy was saying.

Sammy leaned forward, resting his elbows on his knees and looked directly at Ryan. "The thing is, after we create the standards, we have to keep measuring them through our surveys to see if they are working the way we want them to. We have to constantly tweak them and improve upon them. The question always has to be, 'how can we get even better'?"

Ryan was listening. "So tell me a little about the process you would recommend to create these standards for all departments?"

"Not all departments, Ryan. Just the direct-contact departments. After that, we can create standards for all staff to follow. Things that everyone will say and do at every customer interaction – hospital-wide. But remember, not everyone will think this is a great idea because some of the standards we will create will be scripted for consistency. This is change for some people, and some people don't change that easily."

"So what do we do with those people?".

"We just have to make sure they have all of the information, Ryan. We have to give them the 'why' and make sure they understand how it will benefit them and the hospital."

"The worthwhile work!" Ryan was almost shouting with his brief 'Aha.'

"That's right, Ryan. We want Bedford Community Hospital to become the Provider of Choice. There's a lot of people out there that we serve and touch, but there's a lot more that we have the capability to serve, if we're just good enough. Your customers, and for that matter, all people, make very passionate judgments about their perception of quality health care. But those judgments are only based on what they know. And what they know is how they were treated – what their experience was like. The technical aspect of health care they expect. They really don't understand the cost and the impact that technology has on their health, they simply expect it. So what we have to do is give them an experience that is better than they expected, beyond their expectations. If we can do that consistently through improving our service, they not only will come back, they will spread the word – become our personal ambassadors so to speak."

"Sounds good to me." Ryan was excited. "What's the process we should go through? Didn't I just ask you that?"

Sammy laughed. "Yes you did, Ryan, but I tend to go off on tangents. Here's how to start. The managers have to get their departments together and track the customer at every interaction within their department. They go through what they are doing and saying now, and then brainstorm on how to improve. They should take a look at the patient satisfaction surveys to make sure they have the standards in place to cover the questions. Here, Ryan. I jotted down an outline for you to follow. Give it to your managers and have them meet with their departments." Sammy handed Ryan a napkin that he had written the outline on.

Ryan took the napkin and gave Sammy a brief stare. "Glad you made it so formal, Sammy."

Ryan looked at the napkin. He could barely read Sammy's writing, but it said:

1. Each department should meet together to discuss the importance of Customer Service Standards.
2. Track the customer (patients, families, friends) at every interaction within the department and beyond.
3. Write down what they are doing and saying now at every interaction.
4. Brainstorm at the possibilities to make each interaction a better experience for our customers.
5. Look at the qualities and perceptions we would like to portray at every interaction and think of different words, phrases and actions we could use to portray the qualities we want our customers to see and hear.
6. Create the step-by-step standards for each of the interactions, including scripting where necessary.
7. Take a look at our patient satisfaction surveys to make sure we have covered all of the basic areas before we look at the additional areas to focus on.
8. Keep all staff involved. Make the standards theirs.
9. After the new surveys come each quarter, track and post the relevant results in each department.
10. Look at the areas you're scoring high in and celebrate the results.

11. Spread what's working well in your department to other departments.
12. Look for problem areas to focus on and improve upon.

Ryan had reached the bottom of the napkin where the words got crowded. He gave Sammy another icy stare and turned the napkin over.

13. Once the departmental service standards are completed, form a committee of staff and managers to create a set of hospital-wide standards for all staff to follow using the same format.
14. Each manager should choose two or three areas of the standards to focus on and improve upon each quarter, otherwise we will focus on too much and no area will improve as much as it could.
15. Make Customer Service part of everyone's job description and evaluation. It is extremely measurable, and it is that important.

Ryan raised his eyebrows. "Very impressive, Sammy, and it makes sense. But I have a question on number 2."

Number 2? Sammy thought. "What does number 2 say?"

"The part where you said to track the customer at every interaction in the department and beyond. What exactly do you mean by beyond."

Sammy just smiled. "Ryan, I'm a big believer in follow-up phone calls to patients wherever possible. I think all Surgery patients, all In-Patients and all Emergency Room patients should receive a follow-up phone call from us asking how everything is going. It gives them an opportunity to ask questions that they may not have otherwise asked, and besides that, it shows that we care. It shows compassion, at least to some of them. One other thing, Ryan; They won't be expecting it."

"Sounds like a very moral and grand idea, Sammy. There's just one problem. We don't have the time."

Sammy frowned. He got up again and started to pace. "A couple things, Ryan. Number one, you do have the time if only the departments involved in these calls would put a very simple, timely process in place. Like I've said before, it's all about processes and improving on them. You can make the time if you schedule it appropriately. The other thing Ryan: If you're serious about improving the experiences for your customers, if you're serious about BCH becoming the Provider of Choice, if your serious about all of that, you will TAKE and MAKE the time. Otherwise, just forget the whole thing and be satisfied being what you'll stay – an average, run-of-the-mill hospital. I guess they're not so bad. After all, there's thousands of them, and you'll be just like them."

"All right, all right, I get the point, Sammy."

"There's one more thing, Ryan."

Ryan rolled his eyes. "What's that, Sammy?

"Thank You cards and Thinking of You cards."

"What!"

"It's another thing that you can do that your competition probably isn't doing. Your Business Office or Admitting can track all new patients to the hospital and once a month send them a card thanking them for choosing BCH. You can also have your Surgery and In-Patient staff send Thinking of You cards to patients after they are discharged. It creates wonderful good will. You just have to make sure that, like the follow-up calls, you have a log book to track and make sure no one is missed."

"That's actually a great idea, Sammy."

Sammy was pleased with himself. "Yes it is," he said smiling. "Really Ryan, great customer service ideas are only limited by your imagination. Get imaginative, and empower your managers and staff to get imaginative. And the great thing is that most of the best ideas out there to make it a better experience for your customers don't cost a cent, or at the very worst, cost very little."

Now it was Ryan's turn to pace. He was really excited. "This is great stuff Sammy! I'm going to call a managers meeting right away."

Sammy pushed his hand out. "Whoa! Whoa! Slow down, Ryan. Remember, we just talked about the goals yesterday and you haven't even got that off the ground yet. One thing at a time! If you push all of this on your managers and their departments at the same time, you'll have what amounts to a mutiny on your hands. Take it slow and do it right. First the goals, then the service standards. It will take you at least a year to put those two things in place if you do it the right way. After that, we can sit down and talk again."

"OK, OK. But does that mean I won't see you again for a year?"

Sammy was sitting at Ryan's desk with his feet propped up. He folded his arms, and said "Don't worry Ryan, I'll be keeping my eye on you. Trust me. And one more thing, Ryan."

Ryan just shook his head. "Here we go again. There's always just one more thing with you, isn't there Sammy. OK, what is it?"

"It's about your meetings. You're always running the meetings. You don't always have to run the meetings, set the agenda and give orders to be in charge – to be the boss. Give some of the other managers a chance. Let them set the agenda and run the meetings. Let them take turns if it is something that they are interested in and knowledgeable about. I guarantee you they not only will appreciate it, it will enhance your authority and image with them in the long run. Just make sure to tell them that you don't want any surprises and to run the agenda and topics by you ahead of time."

Ryan folded his arms and looked down as he was thinking about it. "OK, I'll give it a try."

He looked up at Sammy, but he was gone.

Chapter X: Oh, How Time Flies

Over the next several months, Ryan, the managers and the staff were working extremely hard at putting the processes in place. Ryan had met with his Board to get their approval on the strategic goals for the hospital, and then worked with the managers to guide them on the relevant goals for their departments.

The managers all got their staff involved and set their departmental goals, and even started to put the individual goals in place based on the departmental goals.

It was a long, difficult process for them. No one had ever had to do the goals before, but over time they could see that it made sense.

After about four months, all of the goals were in place, and it seemed to Ryan like things were working fairly well. He could see improvements in certain areas of the departments and a new found passion with many of the managers and staff. The managers were using the appropriate leadership methods that they learned from Sten, and were leading each of their staff on the goals in ways that they probably wouldn't have discovered on their own.

Performance in the departments was better than before and everyone seemed to be sticking to their budgets. Ryan was happy. Maybe Sammy was right, he thought. Thinking about Sammy again, he wondered where he was. Sammy had promised that he would keep an eye on them, and Ryan hadn't seen him at all. Oh well, he thought, I have to keep the bus rolling along. And then he laughed at the thought. It was time to get moving on the service standards. He knew the managers were anxious, although when the latest patient satisfaction surveys came back, they had improved. Significantly.

In the last Board meeting, the Board seemed quite pleased with the new direction of the hospital. They gave Ryan a lot of credit, but he quickly said the managers and the rest of the staff were responsible. He admitted that he had only gotten some good advice from a new friend and that with everything that he decided to implement, it was the managers and the staff that were actually doing the work.

The more Ryan thought about it, the more he realized that morale probably had improved. Staff seemed much more involved and excited about what they were doing. They seemed to be paying more attention to how well they were performing and not just going through the motions. Ryan thought that the goals probably had something to do with it and, besides that, staff knew that they were going to be held accountable for the goals – they were going to be part of the new performance evaluations.

Some of the managers and staff, Ryan knew, were a little impatient. They expected immediate results on the goals. Ryan knew that it just didn't work that way, and he tried to communicate that to them. He also knew that some of the managers expected that they would immediately become superstar managers after the leadership training with Sten, but again he asked them to be patient. After all, this new way of leading staff was also new for the staff. It was important to remember that they also needed to explain to the staff what they were doing and why.

Ryan was pleased with the new ways he was communicating with his managers. He met with them more often and sought out their input before decisions were made. It made them feel a bigger part of the hospital and got them motivated. On top of that, they had good ideas.

Life was good for Ryan Michaels right now. But he did miss Sammy. On to the service standards.

****

It was now almost a year since Ryan last saw Sammy. Oh, how time flies, Ryan thought. But where was Sammy? Ryan had such good news for him. The new standards had been in place for almost three months now, and the staff's excitement during the process even surprised Ryan.

Ryan had just received the latest patient satisfaction surveys and they were better again. He didn't expect results so quickly. Everything he had ever read or heard about implementing standards was that you should not expect any effect on the surveys for up to a year. But here it was, 90 days later and the surveys looked better than they had in a long time. Ryan hoped that it just wasn't a blip on the screen.

Patient count was up in recent months and the finances of the hospital were in better shape than they had been in several years. Ryan knew that all of the focus that was put on the strategic goals – including finance – was a main reason. He also knew that morale right now was very high. Most staff were going that extra mile for the patients and they felt a part of the big picture. They thought it was fun to see the reactions of all of the hospital's customers. Customers. Wow, how things have changed here. We never used to refer to our patients as our customers, but in reality, that's exactly what they are. And now, the staff referred to them that way too.

Ryan had changed too. He couldn't wait to get up and go to work in the morning. It was fun again, and he knew he had become a better boss. His wife, Ellen, liked to refer to him as "The Great Communicator" instead of "The Great Abdicator" like she used to. Ryan had a smile on his face today. Everything was going so well.

How things change, he thought. When he first met Sammy almost three years ago, he was ready to quit his job. Now look at him. On top of the world. But Sammy had broken his promise about "keeping an eye" on him. Almost a year, and no Sammy.

Ryan was walking down the hall thinking all of this when Linda, the Housekeeping Manager, interrupted his train of thought. "Mr. Michaels, can I talk to you for a few minutes?"

"Of course, Linda. I'm just on my way to my office."

Linda was very quiet as they walked to his office. Ryan wondered what was wrong. She was never this quiet.

When they got to Ryan's office, Ryan offered Linda a chair and pulled out a chair from behind his desk and sat across from her. "What's on your mind, Linda?"

Linda was wringing her hands. She was nervous and somewhat hesitant, but she started. "It's Ann and her whole department. They're driving me crazy."

Ryan looked surprised. "You mean Nursing?" What's going on, Linda? That doesn't sound like Ann."

"Well, Mr. Michaels, Nursing is making our job really hard to do. They insist we do some things their way, and it just doesn't work well the way they want us to do it. And besides that, they're supposed to help us with certain things when we're short-staffed and they won't do it. They just tell us that it isn't their job. They think their job is much more important than ours, and that's just not true. When I try to talk to Ann about it, she just sticks up for her staff and tells us to just do our jobs. Mr. Michaels, if things don't change I'm going to start losing some of my staff. They're not happy, and neither am I."

Ryan was sympathetic. "What can I do Linda?"

"Talk to Ann," Linda said almost shouting. "Make her understand."

"Linda, I'm not sure that is the best way to deal with this, but let me give it some thought over the rest of today. We'll talk again tomorrow. And I'm sorry, Linda, that you were put in this situation."

Linda pushed on. She had to get it all out. "That's fine, Mr. Michaels, but you should know it's not just my department having problems with the departments they work closely with. It's a bunch of them. I know you think things are really going well here, and I guess they are a lot better than a year ago with the goals, standards and everything. But for as much as we are stressing the importance of customer service, the service internally isn't very good. There. I said it."

"Thanks for letting me know, Linda. I promise I'll get back to you tomorrow."

After Linda left, Ryan put his face in his hands and rubbed hard. All that work and things were going the wrong direction all of a sudden. What could he do to make it better? He was at a loss. He kept wondering if it had to do with his leadership, or the leadership in those two departments. After all, he thought, Sten did say that there would be some flat tires along the journey. He couldn't help laughing at that analogy. However, it really didn't make him feel any better. He had to think of something fast.

The conversation with Linda kept Ryan awake that whole night. He had to figure this out, or everyone's efforts during the past year could be for nothing.

Chapter XI: Internally Yours

As Ryan was walking down the hallway to his office the next morning, he couldn't help but notice that the staff wasn't smiling anymore. He did his best to put on a good front, although he didn't feel like smiling either. As he passed staff in the hallway, he greeted them all by name and with a big smile on his face, but all his staff could do was give a weak "hello" and an even weaker smile. Now he was really stressed.

When he walked into his office, he was truly astonished. For the first time since he could remember, he was at a loss for words. Behind his desk with his feet propped up on Ryan's paperwork, there sat Sammy with a big grin on his face.

"How 'ya doin, Ryan? Long time, no see."

"Very funny Sammy." Ryan was not amused. "I'm pretty upset with you Sammy. You promised me that you would keep an eye on things here, and give me some help if I needed it, and you haven't shown up in almost a year. I really am not amused by you just showing up here like everything's OK, because it's not."

"First of all Ryan, I promised you that I would keep an eye on you, and I have. And now you're having a few flat tires, and I'm here."

"Flat tires? Those are the same words that Sten used."

"I know," Sammy smiled. "You know what they say about great minds thinking alike."

Ryan took a deep breath. "You know, Sammy, things were really going well here until the last day or so. Now there seems to be a problem with some of the departments not getting along, and I'm not sure what to do about it. I guess I am glad that you showed up – finally." Ryan's eyes widened and he looked right at Sammy. "Come to think of it, you always seem to show up just at the right time. You're truly amazing. How do you do it?"

Again, Sammy just smiled and said, "I told you I was keeping my eyes on you and I meant it. I have my sources. Let me guess. You're having problems with the internal customer service here. Your departments aren't giving each other what they need to do their jobs, they are not communicating enough and it's starting to cause morale problems. Does that about sum it up?"

"Exactly!" Ryan was truly amazed. How did this guy do it?

Sammy started in. "What these departments have to understand, Ryan, is that their work greatly affects other departments, and if they aren't doing that work as effectively as they could be, it affects those other department's ability to do their job. When that happens, then those other departments will have a difficult time delivering their work effectively to the departments that they affect. It can become a vicious cycle if something isn't done about it."

"Huh?" was all Ryan could manage to get out.

"Let me put it this way, Ryan. Too many times, the departments think that the work – the service – that they are delivering to other departments is just fine, because those other departments aren't telling them any differently. But what happens is that if the service isn't good enough they will complain to everyone else BUT the people who really need to know. And the more that happens, the more resentment comes in to play and that, my dear friend, is the start of what I like to call morale slippage."

Sammy had Ryan's attention again. "So what do we do?"

"It's actually very simple, Ryan. Process, process, process. Just like everything else, without a process in place, good ideas just come and go. You have to have something solid in place to hold the departments accountable. Once you do that, it also should become a part of the manager's performance evaluation."

"So, what's the process you recommend Sammy?"

"It's so simple you'll wonder why you didn't think of it yourself. It's called communication. It's called internal customer service. It's called doing the right thing to improve your patient-focused processes between departments, and the ultimate winners in this whole thing are your customers. Better internal customer service will cultivate better external customer service."

"So," Ryan asked, "how would you define internal customers when we're talking about other departments?"

"Simple, Ryan. An internal customer is another department who you affect with the work that you give them."

"But Sammy, I can make a case that all departments affect all other departments."

"That's true," Sammy said pointing at him, "but we have to get more specific than that. The departments have to discover who their main internal customers are. Who do they affect the most.

Let's take Lisa's department in the Lab. Does Lab affect Nursing? Does Lab affect the Business Office?"

"Well of course they do", Ryan said. "By the way, how do you know Lisa?"

"I told you I had my sources."

Ryan just shook his head. "I think I understand now. The departments have to sit down and figure out who these main internal customers are, and then what?"

"Ryan, in a perfect world, we'd simply ask them how we're doing. But with time being such a factor, I would recommend – at least to start – that each department customize their own questionnaire listing all of the 'services' they provide and not only ask how they are doing with those services, but how they could make the other departments job easier. The question should be 'how can we serve you better than ever before?' or even 'do you have some realistic suggestions of how we could improve our service to you'?"

"And the result?"

"I think you'll find that you will get process adjustments. Tweaking. And another thing Ryan, you must remind the departments if you decide to go ahead with this that it's all about better patient-focused processes. You have to keep personalities out of it. That's the job of the managers to make sure that when these questionnaire are filled out – and they should be filled out by the entire department together – one questionnaire – that you keep it process-focused. Tell them that you will hold each of them accountable to make sure the questionnaires are about jobs and processes, not personalities and attitudes. Personalities and attitudes – if you remember from your leadership development with Sten – are dealt with at a different time by the managers. And they should be dealt with immediately when it happens, not six months later."

"So what happens when the departments get the questionnaire back?"

"Then the fun begins, Ryan. When all of the questionnaires are back from the other departments, the manager should call a meeting for their entire department to go over the questionnaires. The best thing that could happen is some good suggestions on improving processes. I mean, who better to ask than the people receiving your work? Right? But Ryan, here's where you also have to be careful. Just because another department has a suggestion that will make things easier for them doesn't mean you're going to do it. The entire department has to ask themselves some serious questions before you act."

"Such as?"

"Such as 'What are the obstacles that would get in the way and how do we deal with them?' Such as 'Have they made a case how this suggestion would ultimately benefit the patient?' And then the big question: 'How much will this cost and is it in our budget?"

"Sammy, what if a department makes a suggestion and, for whatever reason, it's something that the other department just can't do? Then what?"

"Equally as simple, my friend. Follow-up. The departments must remember that no matter what the result is, they must follow-up with the department that is making the request. If the answer is no, then the manager must go to them and say 'I'm sorry, but we just can't do that right now, and here's why.' That's what they need to hear – the why part. Everyone thinks they know what's going on in other departments, but they really don't know all the details, and once they explain to them the 'why' part, it may open their eyes a little."

Sammy continued. "Follow-up is key. Even when it's a suggestion that you decide to act on, you need to go to that other department and say 'Thanks for the great idea. We're going to use it, here's what it's going to look like, and here's when we're going to start. Bingo!"

Ryan started to laugh. "What was that last part?"

Sammy cocked his head to the side and said, "You mean Bingo. Ahh, Ryan, that's just one of my favorite words, that's all."

Ryan sighed deeply. "Sammy, you've really thrown a lot at me this morning. Can you write me some kind of outline for all of this? Or something?"

Sammy stood up and grabbed a sheet of paper on Ryan's desk. "Way ahead of you friend. Here it is right here." Sammy handed Ryan a sheet of paper with both sides full.

Ryan took it from Sammy and started to look at it. He couldn't help but think that at least it wasn't a napkin this time. It was fairly detailed:

1. As an entire department, determine who our main internal customers are.
2. Develop a questionnaire unique to your department. List all of the things you do in your department and ask them to check all that apply. Find out how you are doing and how you can serve them better than ever before. As time (years) go on and we get more comfortable with the process, move to direct communication with this process. Make sure to put a deadline on returning it – 30 days is usually enough time.
3. When the deadline comes, go to the departments that haven't returned the questionnaire (yes, there will be a few), and ask them to please get it back as soon as possible.
4. When you are on the receiving end of the questionnaire, meet as an entire department to fill it out – one questionnaire per department. Come to a consensus on the content.
5. When you get all of them back, meet as an entire department to go over them.
6. When you get suggestions to consider, ask yourself:
   a. What are the obstacles that may get in the way and how do we deal with them?
   b. Is the suggestion ultimately patient-focused?
   c. Are there costs involved and if so, is it in our budget?
   d. Walk in the Shoes?

7. If you decide to move ahead with a different method of delivering our service to another department, form a plan and determine how to measure the success.
8. Set goals based on that plan.
9. Communicate the decision of your department to the affected department.

10. Consistently follow-up with the department to make sure the plan is working like it should. Tweak if necessary.
11. When possible, visualize the progress of the process change.
12. Repeat number 1 through number 11 in six months.
13. Departmental accountability requires that a Quality Improvement document be completed by each Department Manager throughout this process and submitted to the Quality Improvement Committee. The document will indicate:
    a. When questionnaires were sent out.
    b. Which departments they were sent to.
    c. Results and action taken.

Ryan studied the outline in detail. It looked like a lot of work, but he thought he would give it a try. He had to do something.

"This is really detailed, Sammy, but I have one question."

"Just one?" Sammy was laughing. Sammy laughed a lot, it seemed. "What is it?"

Ryan paged his finger down the outline and stopped. "Number 6D, Walk in the Shoes. What is that?"

Sammy stood up again and started to look out the window. What a great day for golf, he thought. Then he remembered that he was just fooling himself. He really didn't like to dwell on the reality of everything that was actually going on, but he could remember, couldn't he? He scratched his arm again and walked back to where Ryan was sitting.

"Actually Ryan" he started, "a limited Walk in the Shoes program throughout this whole process can be really beneficial on a few fronts. Here's the way it could work. If a department gets a questionnaire back that has a recommendation on it that they're just not sure of, they could get a team member from their department to ask if they could shadow someone in that department during a busy time. That person could look for whatever the recommendation was and see if it would be beneficial or not. Then they could report their finding back to the rest of the team. It's also good in the sense that the person doing the shadowing usually comes back with a new respect for that department. It's human nature to think that we all have the best department, or that we work harder than the other departments. But, in fact, we know that's not true. We all contribute. We all have a role, and again Ryan, we all do worthwhile work."

Ryan looked down at the outline again and said, "Thank you so much Sammy. You did it again. You've really helped pull me out of a jam."

But of course, when Ryan looked up, Sammy was nowhere to be seen. Well, this is sure par for the course, Ryan thought, and then laughed to himself at the comparison. Ryan thought he could still hear that faint scratching sound, but he knew it was his imagination. He also knew that everything Sammy was telling him was something they should have been doing all along. It all made so much sense.

He knew that without Sammy's help, they wouldn't have come as far as they had come. He knew that Sammy was right when he kept pounding in to him that you have to have consistent processes in place for long-term accountability. And he knew that for the first time in years, Bedford Community Hospital was on the right track – or as Sten put it, the right bus.

What Ryan didn't know was that the next year- and-a-half would bring unbelievable change to Bedford Community Hospital.

Chapter XII: The Payoff

As Ryan was driving to the Minneapolis airport to catch a flight to Boston, he had a lot of time to reflect over the past four-and-a-half years. After all, it was almost a three-hour drive from Bedford to Minneapolis. Boring, he thought. Straight roads and cornfields. Then a deer appeared out of nowhere and he had to swerve to avoid hitting it. That certainly woke him up!

Ryan could hardly believe what was happening to him – the reason for this trip. Four years ago he was ready to quit his job as CEO of Bedford Community Hospital. He remembered that day as if it were yesterday. He remembered sitting in his office contemplating his poor performance and the thought of resigning when Sammy appeared – out of thin air, Ryan thought. He always wondered how Sammy was able to do that. Sammy had promised that some day Ryan would know all, but so far at least, he still didn't have a clue how Sammy did it. All he knew was that without Sammy's help, this day would have never come.

Over the past four years, a lot had changed for Ryan and Bedford Community Hospital. From the leadership development and the stubborn pursuit of excellence in leadership by his managers, to the goals and passionate focus on customer service by his managers and most all of the staff. And finally the internal customer service processes that were put in place. It all worked better than Ryan could have ever dreamed of.

The results had been nothing short of remarkable. Almost magical. Two of the strategic goals of BCH were to become the Employer of Choice in Bedford and the surrounding communities and also become the Provider of Choice. Both had happened.

There was a waiting list for employment at BCH. The word had gotten out – it seemed like almost overnight – that BCH was a remarkable place to work. The word was that the staff had fun and that the sense of teamwork was overwhelming. Sure, there was periodic conflict, but the great thing is that the conflicts were resolved almost immediately.

Some of the staff had to go, however. Those decisions were some of the toughest that Ryan had to make, but it had to be done. Those staff had been given every opportunity to get on board with BCH's new culture of teamwork, respect and complete patient focus. Their managers worked with them, evaluated them and asked what they could do to help, but when the change didn't happen, Ryan made the tough decisions.

Change was tough for some people. Even impossible for some others. Ryan had even tried to help some of them find other jobs that they would be happier in. After all was said and done, Ryan believed he had made the right decisions. It was just the right thing to do for all of the rest of the staff and for Bedford Community Hospital.

As Ryan continued to reflect, he still was in awe of the shift in culture and morale. Most all of the staff was completely on board with the changes and were performing beyond their potential in many cases. But Ryan also believed that without the effective leadership from his managers, it wouldn't have happened. Effective leadership, he thought, wasn't that difficult as long as you had a plan. A roadmap. And, of course, it didn't hurt to have mentors like Sammy and Sten. Sure, we all make leadership mistakes, and we always will, but we should learn from those "flat tires." Ryan laughed to himself again at that lame analogy that Sten used way back at the beginning.

The customer service at BCH was extraordinary. Everyone really got on board when the emphasis was placed on quality improvement in the customer service processes and continuous improvement. The Bedford Community Hospital was even recently written up in Health Care Weekly. Their patient satisfaction surveys had gone through the roof and had stayed there. BCH was now at the top of the list in their surveys – they were the standard.

Everyone now looked at their "customers" as an opportunity to go beyond their expectations. Opportunity...what a great word, Ryan thought. They had certainly taken every opportunity to make a difference. Customers were even starting to call BCH the "Magic Kingdom."

The Volunteer Program was nothing short of miraculous. When one of the staff came up with the idea, Ryan had told her to run with it, and just keep Ryan informed of the progress. It had taken her most of the year, but it had been up and running for over nine months. Thirty-seven volunteers. Truly extraordinary for a community the size of Bedford. And the phone calls were coming in weekly of more wanting to volunteer. They acted as escorts to departments, greeters, visitors to patients and more. They would take time to read to the patients if the patient wanted them to, and even play games with them.

The play area for children was a huge hit. And the computers in the waiting area were used constantly by family and friends. The most recent addition was the golf cart. Ryan just shook his head and laughed. He couldn't believe he agreed to that. The hospital had purchased a used golf cart for $500.00 and the volunteers used it to pick up patients who had parked in the handicapped parking areas. That was even written up in the local newspaper, the Bedford Independent.

Financially, the hospital had never been on such sound ground. All departments were keeping their budgets in line and in many cases were significantly under budget. Patient care, he thought was better than at any time in BCH's history, and the average patient census was up 38% from four years ago. Because of all of that, staff and manager salaries were way above the standard for health care. Ryan smiled when he thought that maybe that was also part of the reason they had become the Employer of Choice.

And now the payoff. Ryan still couldn't believe he was headed to Boston to accept the CEO of the Year for health care. The award, in part, was determined by the application that had to be sent by the managers and staff. Ryan hadn't seen the application that his people had sent – he didn't even know that they had gotten together to do it. He was told that the application would be read at the awards ceremony. He did know that it was a very lengthy application and that one part had asked why staff thought their CEO was deserving of it. It also took into account the patient satisfaction surveys, patient count percentages, patient care as determined through interviews with previous patients, and the overall financial condition of the hospital.

Who would have ever believed that this was possible, Ryan thought. He was honored, but very humbled. Tears were streaming down Ryan's face as he approached the airport. He had better be careful he thought. This is a dangerous airport to navigate.

After Ryan had parked his car in the airport parking ramp, he just sat there for a minute with his hands on the steering wheel. He didn't deserve this award, he thought. Sammy did. Sten did. But he didn't. Without their guidance and mentoring, none of this would be possible. He wished they could be here to accept the award with him. He wished that they could at least be here to see what was happening – to see what had happened to the hospital because of their wisdom and advice.

As Ryan got out of his car and grabbed his luggage, he just shook his head. He probably would never see Sammy or Sten again. Over the eighteen months, he had hoped Sammy would show up so he could thank him. But it never happened. As Ryan walked to the terminal, he knew in his own mind that the opportunity would probably not happen. All of a sudden, Ryan was extremely sad. And disappointed. Sammy deserved so much credit.

Chapter XIII: "Thank You Sammy"

While Ryan was waiting to board his plane, he wandered into the gift shop to buy the Minneapolis newspaper. As he was reaching for the newspaper, his eyes were drawn to one of his favorite business magazines. One of the articles promoted on the front cover was "The Top Business Leaders of the '60s." It sounded like a curiously interesting article, so Ryan also bought the magazine. He thought it would pass the time while he was on his long flight to Boston.

Ryan took a seat at his gate and started flipping through the magazine to the article he was interested in. When he got to the page and started looking at the pictures, his heart almost stopped. He froze. He just stared at the picture for a moment with his mouth wide open. There were the goose bumps again.

There, staring right at him was a picture of Sammy – white pony tail, suede fringed jacket and all – leaning against what Ryan could only assume was Sammy's office desk, arms folded with a cigarette in his hand. Smiling right at Ryan.

Below the picture in bold letters was his name: Sammy "Sten" Markson. Ryan started reading the brief bio of Sammy. It said Sammy took his company from the "bottom of the barrel" to the top of its field in four years. The bio went on to say that it was the most significant business turnaround of the decade, and he did it by motivating his staff to get involved, get passionate, and by becoming the "Great Communicator of the '60s." Interviews with some of his former employees said that he was a tough, but very fair boss, and greatly respected by all. He wasn't afraid to make the tough decisions that would benefit the staff and the company in the long run.

Ryan's mind was flooded with questions and wonderment, so he read on. Sammy's middle name – "Sten" – was actually a nickname after his great, great grandpa Stensrud. What he read next brought Ryan to his feet. Apparently, his great, great grandpa Stensrud was one of the founding fathers of a small Midwestern city called Bedford. When Ryan read the last paragraph, it was one of the most shocking and eerie feelings he had ever experienced.

The article ended by saying that after a very sudden and brief illness, Sammy tragically died in 1967 at the height of his career from lung cancer.

Over 40 years ago.

Ryan was stunned. Numbed. He took a deep breath as he was trying to comprehend what he was reading. All he could think of was that Sammy had once told him that some day he would know the truth. But it was impossible, wasn't it. Did it make any kind of sense? No. Was there any logic to it? No.

****

Ryan looked up from the article. He didn't know how it could be possible, but he did know that his meetings with Sammy were as real as anything he had ever experienced. It was starting to make some sense – kind of. Sammy was also Sten, the leadership trainer. Somehow, he made it all happen, Ryan thought in disbelief. All Ryan could do was flop down in his seat, set down the magazine and stare off in to space.

"Wow!" was all he had the energy to whisper.

As Ryan sat there, he was still numb. Stunned. Paralyzed.

Ryan was sure he could feel someone sit down next to him, but when he turned to see who was there, the chair was empty. Ryan was positive in his own mind that he smelled cigarette smoke, and he was positive he heard someone scratching.

Ryan thought for just a moment and then he smiled and turned to the empty chair and said, "You're still trying to quit, aren't you?"

Ryan stared at the empty chair for a moment and then with his face flooding with tears looked up at the sky and said "Thank you Sammy."

"Journey To Becoming An Effective Leader"

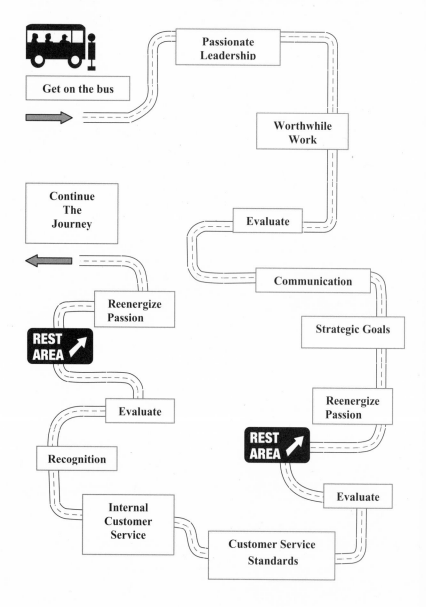

A note from the author:

This was a story about a hospital, but the same lessons about leadership and the processes applied in the story will hold true for most any business or organization. Through Sammy, Ryan Michaels found that there were definite strategies that could help his leadership and his organization improve to become something that went even beyond his expectations:

- **Passionate Leadership:** If you don't feel passionate about what you do and if you don't feel passionate about the mission and vision of your organization, how do your expect your employees to feel? They will model your behavior. If you don't feel that passion, get out! Find something that you **are** passionate about.

- **Worthwhile work:** Not a new concept – these two words have been around a long time. The problem with many organizations is that they don't stress the worthwhile work nearly enough.

- **Communication:** What can I say. There's not enough of it from the top. Employees need information and they need to feel comfortable knowing they can come to their boss to talk.

- **Strategic Goals:** The foundation and lifeblood of every organization.

- **Customer Service Standards:** Every organization that has customers needs standards. They will allow you to consistently improve and go beyond your customers' expectations.

- **Internal Customer Service:** Allows you to focus on teamwork between departments, smoother processes, better attitudes and improved corporate culture and one of the main strategies in becoming the "employer of choice."

- **Recognition:** Without it, none of the above makes any difference.

Great leaders can motivate their staff to extraordinary performance, better teamwork and improved attitudes. Sounds so easy, doesn't it? Of course, it isn't. It takes time, it takes commitment, and it takes passion. More than anything, it takes an overwhelming desire to be the best. I encourage you to start your "journey" today.

Phil Skramstad

Acknowledgments

First of all, I would like to humbly thank Mark Stenson of
Stenson Management Consulting, my friend and mentor. Without Mark,
this book could have never been written, because without his constant
support and encouragement over the years, my career would have never
happened.

I would also like to thank the love of my life – my wife Ellen – who had
to endure months and months of being asked to read and reread every
chapter and in the process, be an objective critic.

Finally, I would like to thank Sammy, who will always live on in my
heart and mind.

Phil Skramstad is president of Imarc Training & Development, Ltd., a leadership and customer service training and consulting company. He also does Conflict Management and Team Building training and development.

Throughout his career, Phil has worked with hospitals and clinics, banks, manufacturing companies and casinos; and with his proactive approach, has guided them in their quest for continuous quality improvement through effective leadership.

Phil lives in the Southwestern Minnesota community of Marshall.

To find out more about Imarc Training & Development, Ltd., go to: imarcltd.com

Sammy's Guide To Customer Service Standards:

1. Each department should meet together to discuss the importance of Customer Service Standards.
2. Track the customer (patients, families, friends) at every interaction within the department and beyond.
3. Write down what they are doing and saying now at every interaction.
4. Brainstorm at the possibilities to make each interaction a better experience for the customers.
5. Look at the qualities and perceptions you would like to portray at every interaction and think of different words, phrases and actions we could use to portray the qualities we want our customers to see and hear.
6. Create the step-by-step standards for each of the interactions, including scripting where necessary.
7. If relevant, take a look at customer satisfaction surveys to make sure you have covered all of the basic areas before you look at the additional areas to focus on.
8. Keep all staff involved. Make the standards theirs.
9. After the new surveys come each quarter, track and post the relevant results in each department.
10. Look at the areas you're scoring high in and celebrate the results.
11. Spread what's working well in your department to other departments.
12. Look for problem areas to focus on and improve upon.
13. Once the departmental service standards are completed, form a committee of staff and managers to create a set of company-wide standards for all staff to follow using the same format.
14. Each manager should choose two or three areas of the standards to focus on and improve upon each quarter, otherwise you will focus on too much and no area will improve as much as it could.
15. Make Customer Service part of everyone's job description and evaluation. It is extremely measurable, and it is that important.

Sammy's Guide To Better Internal Customer Service:

1. As an entire department, determine who your main internal customers are.
2. Develop a questionnaire unique to your department. List all of the things you do in your department and ask them to check all that apply. Find out how you are doing and how you can serve them better than ever before. As time (years) goes on and you get more comfortable with the process, move to direct communication with this process. Make sure to put a deadline on returning it – 30 days is usually enough time.
3. When the deadline comes, go to the departments that haven't returned the questionnaire (yes, there will be a few), and ask them to please get it back as soon as possible.
4. When you are on the receiving end of the questionnaire, meet as an entire department to fill it out – one questionnaire per department. Come to a consensus on the content.
5. When you get all of them back, meet as an entire department to go over them.
6. When you get suggestions to consider, ask yourself:
   a. What are the obstacles that may get in the way and how do we deal with them?
   b. Is the suggestion ultimately customer focused?
   c. Are there costs involved and if so, is it in your budget?
   d. Walk in the Shoes?

7. If you decide to move ahead with a different method of delivering our service to another department, form a plan and determine how to measure the success.
8. Set goals based on that plan.
9. Communicate the decision of your department to the affected department.
10. Consistently follow-up with the department to make sure plan is working like it should. Tweak if necessary.
11. When possible, visualize the progress of the process change.
12. Repeat #1 through #11 in six months.
13. Accountability through Quality Improvement Committee.